Power
of a
New
Life

OTHER BOOKS BY LIONEL WHISTON

Are You Fun to Live With?
Enjoy the Journey
New Beginnings: Relational Studies in Mark
Through Suffering to Victory: Relational Studies in Mark

Lionel Whiston

Power of a New Life

Relational Studies in **Mark**

WORD BOOKS, Publisher, Waco, Texas

First Printing, January 1976
Second Printing, March 1976

CONTENTS

CONTENTS

INTRODUCTION

The Bible comes alive for me as I imagine myself in the place of the various persons and situations in its stories. That is what I would like to do in this series of three books—to compare our own inner lives with the biblical narratives and, by evaluating them in that light, to discover direction and meaning for our living in the contemporary scene.

I have written these studies for those within the Christian tradition. While they are primarily for study groups they may be used for personal study or devotions.

Mark's Gospel portrayed Jesus as the Son of God, Savior and Sovereign of the world, who by his mighty works demonstrated God's unlimited power and grace, and who by his death and resurrection revealed God to be the Giver of victory over sin and death. Jesus was revealed as God's "Man for others" and as "God for us." Emphasis is placed on Jesus' avowed purpose to change, by his teaching and life, the concept of the long anticipated Messiah.

New Beginnings covers Mark 1 through 4:34, ending with the series of parables. *Power of a New Life* begins with 4:35 and a series of miracles around the Sea of Galilee, and ends at 9:50 with Jesus on the way to Jerusalem. *Through Suffering to Victory* goes from Mark 10:1 through 16:8, covering the end of Jesus' ministry, his suffering, death and resurrection. I have omitted 16:9–20, since the most ancient manuscripts do not have these verses which are thought to have been added in the second century.

In going through Mark, I have followed the major divisions outlined by *The Interpreter's Bible* (vol. 7, p. 636). Each study consists of three parts: a Scripture passage (using the Revised Standard Version), comments, and questions. The question sections are detailed at length to help readers do their own thinking. Many questions will not yield a ready answer but are such as need to be lived with.

Since the purpose of these studies is slanted toward relational living, little has been said about historical and social backgrounds, theological implications, biblical scholarship and criticism, important as these are. Rather we have sought to explore Jesus' relationship to himself, his Father and his fellow men, and then consider the same parallel threefold relationship in our own lives.

While I have largely drawn on my own experience of many years in the ministry, I am indebted for many seminal thoughts to Dr. Frederick C. Grant, who wrote on Mark in *The Interpreter's Bible* (vol. 7) and to Dr. Eduard Schweizer, *The Good News According to Mark* (Atlanta: John Knox Press, 1970).

I wish to express appreciation to Phyllis Amidon, George and Joyce Adam and Marilyn Hardy, who have used parts of the manuscript in group study, and to Priscilla Houghton, all of whom have made valuable comments. My son, Dr. Lionel A. Whiston, Jr., of Eden Theological Seminary, has given me the benefit of his rich scholarship and insight. My wife has been a constant inspiration as well as making valued contributions to the book.

ABOUT THIS VOLUME

Power of a New Life leads us intimately into the humanity of Jesus. We see him tired, rejected by his hometown, handling interruptions, playfully fencing with a desperate mother, angry with his disciples and yet ever ready to trust them again. The same Jesus strides in power as these middle chapters of Mark's Gospel reveal his mastery—calming the storm, making the divided mind whole, bringing eternal overtones to local pettiness, courageously facing the shadow of oncoming death and revealing himself as a new kind of Messiah that he demonstrated by his amazing life style. We see Jesus as teacher, healer, Savior, Lord and King.

OUTLINE OF MARK

Volume I   New Beginnings (1–4:34)
   Introduction 1:1–13
   Jesus about the Sea of Galilee 1:13–4:34
      Miracles of healing
      Calling and training of the disciples
      The beginnings of controversy with the Pharisees
      Teachings about the nature of the Kingdom
Volume II   Power of a New Life (4:35–9:50)
   Jesus, by the Sea of Galilee and Wider Journeyings
      Jesus, Lord of life and nature
      More miracles of healing
      The death of John the Baptist
      The tradition of the elders
      The feeding of the multitudes
      Deepening controversy with the Pharisees
      Peter's confession
      The transfiguration and the epileptic boy
Volume III   Through Suffering to Victory (10:1–16:8)
   Jesus in Jerusalem
      Incidents on the way to Jerusalem
      The apocalyptic discourse
      The passion story
      The empty tomb, "He is alive"!

Adapted from *The Interpreter's Bible,* vol. 7, p. 636.

1.
"PUT YOUR HAND IN THE HAND OF THE MAN WHO STILLED THE WATERS"

Mark 4:35–41

(35) On that day, when evening had come, he said to them, "Let us go across to the other side." (36) And leaving the crowd, they took him with them, just as he was, in the boat. And other boats were with him. (37) And a great storm of wind arose, and the waves beat into the boat, so that the boat was already filling. (38) But he was in the stern, asleep on the cushion; and they woke him and said to him, "Teacher, do you not care if we perish?" (39) And he awoke and rebuked the wind, and said to the sea, "Peace! Be still!" And the wind ceased, and there was a great calm. (40) He said to them, "Why are you afraid? Have you no faith?" (41) And they were filled with awe, and said to one another, "Who then is this, that even wind and sea obey him?"

This is the first of a series of miracle stories (4:35–5:43) that occurred near the Sea of Galilee.

We have missed the message in this miracle if the reading of this story makes us wonder why we cannot still storms or control nature. Mark records the signs and wonders of Jesus as a proof that he is the Son of God: God, through Jesus, is breaking through into history. Mark is writing to let us know that he will also break through into our lives in the contemporary scene because Jesus Christ is Lord and his Kingdom will come in power.

Verses 36–37: The fact that Jesus was on board was no guarantee against the threat of storm. He does not promise to keep us out of trouble, but to go with us through trouble. Jesus slept *during* the storm. How often we say, "I'll be glad when this storm is over so I can sleep." It was the conduct of the Moravians on board ship when a violent storm swept the Atlantic that impressed John Wesley. When the storm was at its height and most passengers very sick and frightened, these Christians sang hymns and psalms, rejoicing in God's presence with them. Later Wesley sought them out in London; his heart was "strangely warmed," and he came alive with the love of Christ.

Verse 38: When Mark wrote his Gospel, Jesus was no longer physically present with his people. Yet he really was present as the risen Christ, ready to answer their call. The sleeping Jesus in the boat suggests this paradox: present, yet not present, but within call and ready to respond.

For myself I find that I more frequently call on God for help when I am in critical need than when all is well. It is often true that the more desperate my condition, the more genuine my request, and the more willing and open is my heart to receive and obey him.

Verse 39: I have found the "great calm" in each of two ways. Sometimes prayer has resulted in a change in circumstances, as when the storm at sea lessened. God is truly a God who *changes things*. I have also found that conditions can outwardly remain the same, yet I can have great peace within. An inner reserve of courage and faith I did not even know I possessed is given to help me through the crisis. *I have been changed.* Either way it is God's mighty work and we praise him.

In verse 36 we read, "Other boats were with him." They received the benefit of the stilled waters. There are always many others of whom we have no knowledge that are blessed by the victories that Christ is working out in us.

Verse 40: Jesus chided his disciples for their lack of faith. Exactly how do you overcome fear? Recently I had a heart fibrillation. It straightened out just before breakfast on Sunday morning leaving me quite weak and somewhat dizzy. I was a guest preacher that morning, so I had to go to church. While the local pastor was conducting the service, I was by the pulpit, sitting down during the singing of the opening hymn. I asked God for strength and then said, "Lord, what do you want me to do this morning?"

The thought came, "You are sitting down because you are afraid. Stand up and sing." Although I felt dizzy, I grabbed hold of the pulpit, pulled myself up and started to sing. At first I was shaking and very afraid. But as I sang, I forgot myself and soon felt normal. "Faith is fear that has said its prayers!" Obedience to God's will turns fear into confidence.

To me the miracle was not so much my gaining normal poise and health, as God's confirming of my act of faith. The miracle took place in my heart first. God honored my faith and obedience. The quieted pulse and the physical well-being were the natural results.

Verse 41: Immanual Kant said that two things filled him with awe: the moral law within and the starry universe without. Charles Wesley described his response to God as "lost in wonder, love, and praise." Jesus, the Son of God, is "ruler of all nature."

QUESTIONS

Verse 36: They took him with them. Do you? Think of some recent journeys, plans, programs, outings, contracts, promotions, missions. Did you take Christ with you? Did his Spirit guide and permeate the events? Recall one where "you took Christ."

Verse 37: Do you use God as a Santa Claus, and prayer as magic? Do you think that if Christ is with you, there will be no trouble? Jesus himself did not escape trouble! Meditate on this.

Verse 38: Wherever you are, there is Christ, just a prayer away. A word of entreaty and he is at your side. Do you feel this? Is this your way of daily living? Do you call him when you need him? Do you sometimes not call because you feel guilty that you only call him when in need? Would you want your own child so to feel guilty?

Was Jesus asleep hoping that they would have courage and skill to handle the boat in the storm? Is that why God seems to make himself distant and invisible at times so that we may draw on the inner resources of faith, courage and trust?

Verse 39: Recall an incident when circumstances changed radically as the result of prayer and faith. Recall another where threatening circumstances remained just as perilous, but Christ gave his peace and calm to you—such a peace as passed all understanding (Phil. 4:7).

Verse 40: Christ asks today as then, "Why are you afraid?"—"Why are you so timid?" as Weymouth puts it. God's promise is that we shall not fear. What keeps us from trusting in him? Take time to write down in detail the things that you fear. Face them squarely in the presence and power of God. The love and power of God cast out fear.

Verse 41: A friend of mine said, "If you've seen one mountain, you've seen them all"! Do you get used to the miracles of God? Ralston Young, redcap at New York's Grand Central Station and a great man of faith, and I were looking out of our window toward the east. As the sun came over the horizon he exclaimed with glee, "He's done it again!" How can you cultivate more of this spirit of wonder and awe?

2.
MY AUTOBIOGRAPHY

Mark 5:1–13

(1) They came to the other side of the sea, to the country of the Gerasenes. (2) And when he had come out of the boat, there met him out of the tombs a man with an unclean spirit, (3) who lived among the tombs; and no one could bind him any more, even with a chain; (4) for he had often been bound with fetters and chains, but the chains he wrenched apart, and the fetters he broke in pieces; and no one had the strength to subdue him. (5) Night and day among the tombs and on the mountains he was always crying out, and bruising himself with stones. (6) And when he saw Jesus from afar, he ran and worshiped him; (7) and crying out with a loud voice, he said, "What have you to do with me, Jesus, Son of the Most High God? I adjure you by God, do not torment me." (8) For he had said to him, "Come out of the man, you unclean spirit!" (9) And Jesus asked him, "What is your name?" He replied, "My name is Legion; for we are many." (10) And he begged him eagerly not to send them out of the country. (11) Now a great herd of swine was feeding there on the hillside; (12) and they begged him, "Send us to the swine, let us enter them." (13) So he gave them leave. And the unclean spirits came out, and entered the swine; and the herd, numbering about two thousand, rushed down the steep bank into the sea, and were drowned in the sea.

I am tempted as I read this incident to write about demonology, exorcism, and the pagan beliefs of Jesus' day. It would be less painful to write about these concepts than to be deeply honest with you. For me, these verses are not just a Bible story of a demoniac of two thousand years ago, but they recall the traumatic pilgrimage of my life. I see myself here.

I, too, have lived amid the dead bones of the past, the prisoner of my childhood habits, fettered by my imaginations, and torn asunder by my desires to please scores of different people.

If I had been an extroverted person, I might have exhibited my rebellion in an overt manner, exhibiting physical violence, drunkenness, ill temper, savage words. But I am introverted. I lived a prisoner of my loneliness. My inner moods and fantasies knew no restraint. Jealousy, lust, egotism, subtle plays for power possessed me. Night and day I was in torment. Memories of past thoughts and scenes returned again and again to haunt me.

My relationship to Jesus Christ, like that of the demoniac, was ambivalent. It was not difficult for me to admit with my intellect that he was Jesus, Son of the Most High God, but when he laid claim to my life I resisted him. Like Augustine, I said, "Lord, make me pure, but not now." I refused to be honest with my family and fellow man. My pride forbade it. So I pushed God aside with "Don't torment me. I can't stand it." I preferred the dark corridors of my own thoughts to the pain of being honest about my way of life.

Finally I listened as God called my name, saying, "Lee

Whiston, tell me who and what you really are." I then acknowledged that my name, too, was Legion. I was the prisoner of many moods, the wearer of a myriad masks, the slave of countless imaginations. Which of these was I? I was Legion. But I had never before faced this fact—much less admitted it.

I tried to compromise, for I did not want my sins to be sent too far away. I wanted to reserve the "right" to indulge in my moods and fantasies once in a while. I, too, begged God to let me keep a little sin for occasional solace! But when the torment was ultimately unbearable I consented to let God really take over my life. It was then that he drowned my past in the great sea of his grace.

I wish I could record my life story as a *fait accompli*. But again and again, in new areas and relationships, the battle is repeated. I still know times of acute loneliness. I still resist God's will. But he is faithful, staying by me and always winning me back to him.

QUESTIONS

The challenge of this narrative to our personal lives requires realistic self-knowledge. Will you join me as together we reflect on the implications of this incident and the applications to our own lives? Are there painful memories of the past in your life that have the power to hurt? That refuse to "stay buried"? Nameless and named fears that haunt? Habit patterns that mock you and inspire rebellious behavior? The Spirit of God came in the person of a man named Jesus to speak to the demoniac. The Spirit of the Christ speaks again to each of us today. Let us listen.

He is speaking now. Write down the fears or failures that haunt you. Will you, in surgical honesty, spell out the dreads or forebodings that rise out of the past or future to hold you in their grip? As you do this, it is conceivable that discouragement may settle in on you as you see a host of weaknesses and hurdles to be overcome. But the same power that was in Jesus is available to you today as you are cleansed, freed and empowered in a new wholeness of life in Christ.

Let me suggest three specific steps which I use frequently: First, write a letter to God, telling him in detail the fears and problems that trouble you. Later, write a letter from God (or Christ) to you. Read them through several times for a week and then burn them, giving all of their contents into his keeping. Second, talk everything out leisurely and fully with God in the presence of a trusted friend, and then commit it all to God in audible prayer. Third, talk everything through with a group that you love and trust, throwing yourself on God's and their love, and receiving their supportive love.

3.
PROPERTY VERSUS PERSON

Mark 5:14–20

(14) The herdsmen fled, and told it in the city and in the country. And people came to see what it was that had happened. (15) And they came to Jesus, and saw the demoniac sitting there, clothed and in his right mind, the man who had had the legion; and they were afraid. (16) And those who had seen it told what had happened to the demoniac and to the swine. (17) And they began to beg Jesus to depart from their neighborhood. (18) And as he was getting into the boat, the man who had been possessed with demons begged him that he might be with him. (19) But he refused, and said to him, "Go home to your friends, and tell them how much the Lord has done for you, and how he has had mercy on you." (20) And he went away and began to proclaim in the Decapolis how much Jesus had done for him; and all men marveled.

Verses 14–17: Mark's Gospel is the story of the mighty acts of God performed through Jesus. People flocked to see these happenings. Our churches today can also display the mighty acts of God through the risen Christ to his people. As we let his power become effective in us, churches will become centers of "happenings" and continuing miracles.

What a surprising reaction there was to the healing of the demoniac! People had grown so accustomed to his wild behavior that they were actually afraid to see him, a sane, healed man, sitting beside Jesus. His insanity was easier to cope with than his sanity! They begged Jesus to leave their area. The owners would rather have the demoniac raving amid the tombs again, if only it would bring back their pigs! One man is not worth two thousand pigs!

This attitude is prevalent even today. We forget that many social ills have their basis in economic pressures and greeds. The battle over ecology often centers on property versus persons, profits versus public health. The United States is taking strenuous steps to increase its armament exports and selling billions of dollars' worth of war material in order to gain a favorable balance of trade. When India and Pakistan fought each other, both sides used United States weapons. Must we balance our national accounts at the cost of the blood of humanity? We are so accustomed to armaments, bombs and war that we would feel threatened in a land where peace was protected only by good will. The sanity of peace and love is harder to take than the insanity of the arms race!

Is it right that migrant workers go underpaid, poorly housed, their children having the highest illiteracy of any group in our country in order that we may have cheaper food? Did you join the grape and lettuce boycott? If Jesus were here would he speak of these things?

Verses 18–19: How often the Spirit of Jesus suggests "Go home to your friends and tell them . . ." Often when a young businessman is converted or finds newness of life in Christ, he feels he should go to a theological seminary and study to be a minister, when the Master is really saying, "Go home. Live a new quality of life in your business. Introduce the Christ Spirit there. Live this new life with your wife and children." Home is always the hardest place to live for God and the place we are most apt to grow careless.

One of my greatest regrets as I review my last pastorate before retiring was that I worked so wholeheartedly among my church people and community and accepted many outside speaking engagements but did practically nothing to be helpful in a prison which was only three miles away. In the last twelve months, there have been riots, burnings and murders there. Would things have been different if a score of my men and I had gone to this prison and formed Bible classes and started a small corps of changed lives and thus introduced a new spirit into that prison?

Verse 20: The man disobeyed Jesus. He announced what Jesus had done throughout the neighborhood. In spite of this, God used his disobedience, but he could have used his obedience to even greater advantage!

QUESTIONS

Verses 14–15: What changes are taking place in your life? A daughter told me that she had resented tending to her aged, incontinent father, but she was so changed by a new dedication to Christ that she lovingly cared for him, and embraced him fondly and later was greatly re-warded by his grateful responses to her love. What changes have you experienced in yourself and seen in others because of Christ's power?

The Thessalonians said of the early Christians, "These men . . . have turned the world upside down" (Acts 17:6). In reality they were putting it right side up. Describe the way in which Jesus has turned your life "right side up," how he has brought sanity into your life. Contrast the insanity of the days of fear, worry, self-will.

Verses 16–17: What are the places in your life where property and personal values clash? What things tend to take precedence over personal values? Rigid program? A passion for orderliness? Appearances? Furniture? Property? Promotions? Pay increases?

What does the Spirit of Christ say to you about pollution, strip mining, racial discrimination, the millions of illiterate and underfed children in these United States, the one-third of the world that goes to bed hungry every night? Do you see any way in which God is wanting you to get your teeth into one of these problems, or similar ones in your community? Is God pointing you to some place of service very close to home that you have over-looked? What responsibility has the Christian toward solving these problems? Ask God to show you what one person, fully dedicated to God, can accomplish. Remember, "One man can try."

Verse 19: Describe the difficulties of living the new life style at home and on the job. Why is it often easier to do this among strangers? Note that the command is not to go home and give advice, judge or convert people, but just to tell what God has done for you and of his great love. Are you doing this by the radiance and overflow of a new love in your life? Share your thoughts about this.

4.
JESUS, LORD OF LIFE AND DEATH

Mark 5:21–24a, 35–43

(21) And when Jesus had crossed again in the boat to the other side, a great crowd gathered about him; and he was beside the sea. (22) Then came one of the rulers of the synagogue, Jairus by name; and seeing him, he fell at his feet, (23) and besought him, saying, "My little daughter is at the point of death. Come and lay your hands on her, so that she may be made well, and live." (24) And he went with him. . . .

(35) While he was still speaking, there came from the ruler's house some who said, "Your daughter is dead. Why trouble the Teacher any further?" (36) But ignoring what they said, Jesus said to the ruler of the synagogue, "Do not fear, only believe." (37) And he allowed no one to follow him except Peter and James and John the brother of James. (38) When they came to the house of the ruler of the synagogue, he saw a tumult, and people weeping and wailing loudly. (39) And when he had entered, he said to them, "Why do you make a tumult and weep? The child is not dead but sleeping." (40) And they laughed at him. But he put them all outside, and took the child's father and mother and those who were with him, and went in where the child was. (41) Taking her by the hand he said to her, "Talitha cumi"; which means, "Little girl, I say to you, arise." (42) And immediately the girl got up and walked; for she was twelve years old. And immediately they were

overcome with amazement. (43) And he strictly charged them that no one should know this, and told them to give her something to eat.

We will deal with verses 24b–34 later. We are excerpting them so as to treat the two healings separately and in their entirety.

Verse 22: Jairus is willing to break with tradition. He is a man of prestige appealing to an itinerant rabbi. How much we are willing to do when pleading for another! To what limits we go when in dire extremity! We relinquish our prejudices.

Verse 23: There is tenderness in the words, "My little daughter." The Phillips translation says, "My little girl." Jairus shows great faith in Jesus; more so than most of Jesus' fellow Jews. Were stories of Jesus' healing touch being told from person to person?

Verses 33–36: "Your daughter is dead." What finality was here! Nothing more could be done! This usually sensitive Listener by-passes the statement and repeats the sentence he spoke so often, "Do not fear, only believe." These words, "Fear not," were frequently spoken immediately before some mighty act of God: to Joshua before entering the Promised Land, to the shepherds at the birth of Jesus, to the woman when his resurrection was announced. Here again, when people had given up hope God was about to perform a mighty act through Jesus.

The world lives in fear of death, bows before its inevitability. We tell only half the story when we say, "He died." God in Jesus broke through the finality of death and makes us inheritors of eternal life. He said, "Because I live, you will live also." Jesus is both Lord of life and Lord of death. Man says that in the midst of life we are with death, but Jesus says that in the midst of death we are with life—victorious, eternal life.

Verses 37–43: Ridicule is harder to take than downright opposition or persecution. Jesus' heart must have ached for these people who knew so little of the power and love of his Father. He excluded the curious, and those whose lack of faith or downright opposition would be a hindrance. "He took her by the hand." Again he touches the one in need. The tenderness of that touch and those words! The mighty work is immediate. Faith and love brought it about.

This story is narrated by Mark in order that we may believe that nothing is impossible with God. Sin and death are man's archenemies; God in Christ conquers both. One can be on his own deathbed or stand by that of a loved one and through Christ face the finality of physical death, and yet have faith that in Christ there is a resurrection when as a new creature each of us enters into eternal life with him.

QUESTIONS

Verses 22–23: Discuss some situation where, like Jairus, out of emotional urgency you have broken through patterns of traditional behavior or made some bold or unusual overture or request. Under what circumstances and why did you do it? What happened? What happened to you?

Does the phrase "the touch of Jesus" have a rich and warm sacramental meaning for you? The gospel song "He touched me" brings a strong message. Talk of occasions when you feel that he touched you. Was it affirming, empowering? Were there times of stern discipline in his touch? Talk of these, too.

Verse 24: He went with him. Jesus is always our traveling companion. Every road can be an Emmaus journey. (See Luke 24:13–35.) Describe one such journey.

Verses 35–36: Speak of a time of finality in your life, when it seemed as though you could not go on, as though the lights had gone out forever. Describe how the lights came on again! How did the words, "Fear not, only believe" come alive for you?

Verse 37: Do you share the deep and tender experiences of your life with others? Jesus took three disciples and the parents into the child's room. Do you share wedding and funeral experiences with children? Take them with you to visit the grandparents? Include them in family financial discussions? The news of a coming operation? Let them join with you in faith and prayer about it?

How could ministers let laymen be a greater part of the pastoral responsibilities? How can you let others share more deeply in the significant experiences of your life?

Verses 38–43: Twenty years ago the doctors told my wife she had pernicious anemia and had only a few months to live. She was on the edge of coma. Together we thanked God for our thirty-five years of marriage. She outlined the program that she would like at her memorial service. We prayed together and thanked God —quite unknowing that he had a miracle in store for us: her complete recovery. To face death with Christ is to find resurrection and the joy of eternal living.

How do you feel in the presence of death? The death of others? The approaching death of yourself? Are you preparing for the final death by lesser deaths each day such as the giving up of pride? The death of self-will? The sacrifice of indulgent desires? Has each "little death" been prelude to a "little resurrection" with newness of joy in victory over self and sin? Speak of this. Are you confident as you face your final death that in Christ it becomes resurrection in him?

5.
INTERRUPTIONS

Mark 5:24b–34

(24b) And a great crowd followed him and thronged about him. (25) And there was a woman who had had a flow of blood for twelve years, (26) and who had suffered much under many physicians, and had spent all that she had, and was no better but rather grew worse. (27) She had heard the reports about Jesus, and came up behind him in the crowd and touched his garment. (28) For she said, "If I touch even his garments, I shall be made well." (29) And immediately the hemorrhage ceased; and she felt in her body that she was healed of her disease. (30) And Jesus, perceiving in himself that power had gone forth from him, immediately turned about in the crowd, and said, "Who touched my garments?" (31) And his disciples said to him, "You see the crowd pressing around you, and yet you say, 'Who touched me?'" (32) And he looked around to see who had done it. (33) But the woman, knowing what had been done to her, came in fear and trembling and fell down before him, and told him the whole truth. (34) And he said to her, "Daughter, your faith has made you well; go in peace, and be healed of your disease."

Here Jesus was interrupted again. One wonders whether his life was anything but a constant series of interruptions! We are amazed at his patience and serenity. He seemed to be always ready for the person in need. Jairus must have been very impatient at this interruption with his daughter at death's door. Jesus must have felt for Jairus. Yet he gave of himself fully to the healing of this woman.

Verse 30: There is tiredness of the body from physical exercise, a weariness of the mind from grappling with mental problems, and an exhaustion of soul from pouring out love and healing. No one of us can continuously give out without feeling spent. No one can vicariously carry the sins and handicaps of others without knowing the feeling of spiritual exhaustion.

A nurse told me that before the enrichment of her life through Christ, she could give ten or fifteen backrubs with little sense of fatigue. But now she feels that her hands are as the hands of God. The risen Christ is touching people through her. So many speak to her now about her ministrations, and conversations on a deep level, once so rare, are a common occurrence. "But," she says, "I come away spent, exhausted, and have to take a little time with the Lord to be refilled again, even if it is only during the few seconds as I walk down the corridor to another room."

Verses 31–34: Jesus could easily have gone on with Jairus after verse 29, for the woman was already healed, but there remained the delicate and gracious encounter by which the personhood of this timid, retiring woman needed to be affirmed and her sense of identity assured. "The woman [came] scared and shaking all over" (Phillips). She asked no recognition. She hoped to leave unnoticed. This timid soul needed assurance.

With what gentleness Jesus must have looked at her. His manner made it easy for her to tell him "the whole truth." The confession freed her soul. Then came that warm address, "Daughter." Jesus claimed no credit for what had happened. He gave her the credit as he said, "It is *your faith* that has healed you" (Phillips). He had enabled her to make her confession and to speak out before the crowd. He had affirmed her. Now she must have felt a sense of importance. There had been a healing of spirit as well as body. She left with a stronger self-image.

QUESTIONS

Verses 24b–27: Jesus was answering an emergency call. It was a matter of life or death. This woman interrupted him. How do you handle interruptions? Take them in stride or blow your top? Would it help to ask the question, "Which is more important, my plans or the other person's need?" Do interruptions largely trouble us because our program and the opportunity to fulfill our ego have been thwarted?

Have you tried this little prescription: "See the interrupter in terms of his needs and not in terms of his faults"? A member of the family comes home late, or has an accident, breaking a dish or crumpling a car fender. Can you see needs rather than faults? To emphasize another's faults is to diminish a person. To see and meet his needs is to enhance and affirm him.

Verse 28: How strong is our faith and expectation as

we approach God? Earlier Mark wrote of the faith of the four who bore the paralytic to Jesus (2:3–5). Here it was the faith of the invalid herself. We feel her desperation and earnestness, a hungering and thirsting! Are we sufficiently earnest? Sufficiently desperate? Discuss this.

Our approaches to people vary with our temperaments. Jairus came in a straightforward manner, face to face. This woman came shrinking, probably hoping not to be noticed. Both had much faith. How do you approach God? Boldly (Heb. 4:16, KJV)? Timidly ("If you will . . ." 1:40)? And yet with faith? Do you find yourself approaching people with attitudes similar to those with which you approach God? Does your attitude need to be changed or do you feel comfortable with it?

Verse 30: Tell of an experience when you felt "power going forth from" you. If this is not a frequent experience, ask yourself, "Do I care enough? Listen with sufficient attention? Vicariously suffer with others so that their pain or loneliness becomes mine? Do I spend myself in intercessory prayer?"

Verses 32–34: Can you meet another's need in such a way that the recipient becomes a stronger person? Gifts can weaken one, leaving him dependent, and feeling inferior. Do you try to do favors and bestow gifts, whether physical or spiritual, in such a way as to affirm the personhood of the recipient? Give an example of where this happened—or failed to happen.

Is your touch a healing touch or a weakening one? Do people tend to become more dependent on their own inner resources as the result of your touch and/or help?

6.
JESUS AND HIS HOMETOWN

Mark 6:1–6

(1) He went away from there and came to his own country; and his disciples followed him. (2) And on the sabbath he began to teach in the synagogue; and many who heard him were astonished, saying, "Where did this man get all this? What is the wisdom given to him? What mighty works are wrought by his hands! (3) Is not this the carpenter, the son of Mary and brother of James and Joses and Judas and Simon, and are not his sisters here with us?" And they took offense at him. (4) And Jesus said to them, "A prophet is not without honor, except in his own country, and among his own kin, and in his own house." (5) And he could do no mighty work there, except that he laid his hands upon a few sick people and healed them. (6) And he marveled because of their unbelief. And he went about among the villages teaching.

Verse 1: Jesus' ministry had been largely around Lake Galilee and in Capernaum. Now he moves in the wider circle of Galilee. Jesus' "own country" was Nazareth, yet he did not feel at home here. His home was with any who did the will of God (see 3:35).

Verses 2–3: It was the custom of the Jews in their synagogues to invite any visiting rabbi to speak. The people recognized Jesus' wisdom and mighty works, yet they took offense! Jealousy could have been the root of their rejection, so they set about "boxing him in" by referring to him as "the carpenter." We can always diminish a person by using some generic term. He's that German, that black, that English guy, that salesman. To call Jesus a carpenter was to assert that he was not a scholar. Therefore, what he said could not be of much value. The brothers and sisters were average people, therefore Jesus must be average, too!

Verse 5: Could do no mighty works is a strong statement. It shows how much God depends on our faith and cooperation. In the two mighty works we have just considered (5:21–43) Jesus placed high value on the faith of those who took the initiative in coming to him.

Verse 6: Jesus marveled at their unbelief. It is always a cause for amazement when we, who see the daily miracles of God, are confronted with people in our own homes or churches who, though seeing the same events, cannot see the hand of God in them.

The unfaith of his townspeople, former playmates and school friends must have cut him to the quick, but it did not dampen his spirit nor affect his determination to go forward. He talked about a prophet being without honor only among his own countrymen and then moved on, undaunted, to teach in other villages.

QUESTIONS

Verses 1–3: Do you find it harder to relate to your

home folks? I personally find it easier to pray and speak of God's love with others than to those closest to me. What is your experience? Do you tend to downgrade people from your own family, hometown or church with something like "I knew him when . . ."? Do you "take offense," look patronizingly upon those who were once children in your neighborhood? Does familiarity breed contempt?

Verse 5: Lack of faith on the part of the people of Nazareth hampered Jesus. On the contrary, our faith can be a strong help to God today in bringing the Kingdom into being either through individual or corporate change. Think of situations where you have had faith in people. What has happened? Are there some people in your family, or church, or community that you have given up on? By whom you are turned off? Because of their belonging to another political, racial or religious group or another era? Speak of places where you have faith in spite of the above differences.

Verse 6: Can you proceed with your work unperturbed if others lack faith in you? Talk about this.

Have you thought of the power that your faith can give to another's life, particularly to someone in your own home? A woman was elected president of the teachers association of her city school system. There were important and threatening issues at stake. She was desperately afraid and asked God's help. While praying it came to her that as a first-year high school student she had been asked to lead her youth group one Sunday evening. She came afraid to her mother who said, "Ruth, you can do that. I know you can. Go ahead; God is with you."

Now thirty-five years later the Holy Spirit brought again her mother's faith to her. "You can do that, Ruth." She went forward and did it, strengthened by the faith of another. Tell of how you are believing in people around you, strengthening them, affirming them by little acts of faith.

7.
DELEGATING TASKS

Mark 6:7–13

(7) And he called to him the twelve, and began to send them out two by two, and gave them authority over the unclean spirits. (8) He charged them to take nothing for their journey except a staff; no bread, no bag, no money in their belts; (9) but to wear sandals and not put on two tunics. (10) And he said to them, "Where you enter a house, stay there until you leave the place. (11) And if any place will not receive you and they refuse to hear you, when you leave shake off the dust that is on your feet for a testimony against them." (12) So they went out and preached that men should repent. (13) And they cast out many demons, and anointed with oil many that were sick and healed them.

Verse 7: The disciples of Jesus recognized and obeyed him as their leader. He called them; they came. He sent them out; they went. Undoubtedly they were hesitant and uncertain, but they acted with trust and obedience.

Jesus trained his disciples so that they could function after he had gone. John's imprisonment could well have reminded Jesus that his own death was near. Hence this necessity for "laboratory training" for those who were to carry on his work.

There is much wisdom in going two by two. Each

feels the supportive love of the other. The two can talk over the day's happenings, reflect on them and pray together. There can be mutual encouragement and evaluation of mistakes.

Jesus not only taught, but trained his disciples to teach; not only exorcized demons, but gave them authority to do the same. It was my tendency in the pastorate to try to do ten men's work rather than train ten men to do the work. How much wiser Jesus was! He trusted others with his work, even though they might not do it as well as he could have done.

"Demon possession" is to be possessed by or dominated by evil to an uncontrollable degree. Childhood patterns of self-will and tantrums, compulsive gambling, uncontrolled lust for power or money or sex either in imagination or in deed, alcoholism, an uncontrolled temper, being victimized by fears, gnawing loneliness and self-pity . . . all of these would have been called demon possession in Jesus' day. Jesus gives to his disciples today, as then, power to have victory over these evils.

Verses 8–9: They were to travel light. Some men have taken verse 8 literally. It is amazing how God has honored this quality of daring and provided for the needs of such followers. I thank God for such men. I find myself in this modern age behaving very differently. The day after writing this I shall be flying from Boston to Kansas to lead in a week's conference. I shall be taking quite a good-sized bag of clothing and two hundred dollars for plane fare! However, I know very well the difference between undue trust in these material conveniences and dependence on the Lord. I need to exercise discipline and stewardship in regard to material possessions. I also need to "travel light" in the spirit!

Verses 10–11: The disciples were to let God guide them to the place they felt he had for them and then to stay there and not shop around for hosts more congenial or a house more comfortable. The work and not the surroundings had top priority.

If the disciples had done their best and people still would not receive them, they were to forget this incident (i.e., shake off the dust of the past), and move on to the next assignment.

Verses 12–13: The disciples went out confidently under the authority that Jesus had given them. It was in his name and through his power they preached, overcame evil, and brought healing and peace.

Man does not reach his fulfillment until he has found an authority that he can obey. He is primarily creature, not creator. Much as he might like to play God in the pursuit of riches or power, he is made to obey God, the God we know through Jesus. Obedience to God brings fulfillment. We sense this fulfillment in verse 30.

QUESTIONS

Verse 7: Are you seeking to train others in the Kingdom work? Are you more eager to work and witness yourself than to help others do this? Do you have spiritual children? Spiritual grandchildren? Are you a reproducer of reproducers?

Verses 8–9: Are you traveling light or are you over-loaded with too heavy a program? Worried and fretted about finances, health, security? Is your journey ponderous and plodding? Or joyous with lightness of heart? What excess baggage are you carrying? Do you find your security and trust resting in money, things, people's approval? What can you do about this?

Verses 10–11: Tell of times when in uncomfortable lodgings or surrounded by inhospitable environment you have had inner victory and let your gratitude and joy be your witness. Can you be rejected and yet not be discouraged from making further effort? Can you move on to the next task with good spirit? Give an instance of where you did or did not do this.

Verses 12–13: Jesus sent his disciples out into action. He is doing the same today. Not all are to preach, cast out demons or heal with oil. But all of us as Christians are under the authority of Jesus Christ. Do you feel empowered by him, and that you are being obedient to him, as you diaper a baby, instruct an employee, work in an office, in a research laboratory or help a lame man across the street? Talk of what it means to you to be commissioned or sent out day by day by Jesus Christ.

God offers each of us, through Christ, authority over evil. He asks us to partake in the power of his resurrection. What is your experience? When you encounter an alcoholic husband, a stubborn child, a dishonest, greedy merchant, a "road hog," do you react angrily and let evil master you? Do you let the power and love of God through Christ enable you to oppose evil and to triumph over it, even defeat it, by love? Tell of your experience.

Remember the old days when you learned to swim? You were always assigned a buddy! Do you, like these pairs of disciples and like Paul, have a spiritual buddy, a confidant? A teammate with whom to pray and to work? Someone with whom you can share your problems and mistakes, someone to give you affirmation and supportive love? If not, will you let God guide you to someone?

8.
WHEN DO YOU BREAK A PROMISE?

Mark 6:14–29

(14) King Herod heard of it; for Jesus' name had become known. Some said, "John the baptizer has been raised from the dead; that is why these powers are at work in him." (15) But others said, "It is Elijah." And others said, "It is a prophet, like one of the prophets of old." (16) But when Herod heard of it he said, "John, whom I beheaded, has been raised." (17) For Herod had sent and seized John, and bound him in prison for the sake of Herodias, his brother Philip's wife; because he had married her. (18) For John said to Herod, "It is not lawful for you to have your brother's wife." (19) And Herodias had a grudge against him, and wanted to kill him. But she could not, (20) for Herod feared John, knowing that he was a righteous and holy man, and kept him safe. When he heard him, he was much perplexed; and yet he heard him gladly. (21) But an opportunity came when Herod on his birthday gave a banquet for his courtiers and officers and the leading men of Galilee. (22) For when Herodias' daughter came in and danced, she pleased Herod and his guests; and the king said to the girl, "Ask me for whatever you wish, and I will grant it." (23) And he vowed to her, "Whatever you ask me, I will give you, even half of my kingdom." (24) And she went out, and said to her mother, "What shall I ask?" And she said, "The head of John the baptizer." (25) And she came in immedi-

ately with haste to the king, and asked, saying, "I want you to give me at once the head of John the Baptist on a platter." (26) And the king was exceedingly sorry; but because of his oaths and his guests he did not want to break his word to her. (27) And immediately the king sent a soldier of the guard and gave orders to bring his head. He went and beheaded him in the prison, (28) and brought his head on a platter, and gave it to the girl; and the girl gave it to her mother. (29) When his disciples heard of it, they came and took his body, and laid it in a tomb.

Four main characters are featured in this story; a fearless prophet, a vain king, an avenging woman, an innocent pawn. Can we see ourselves in these people?

John the Baptist was fearless in his denunciation of sin and sinners. Like Amos, he placed the plumbline of righteousness alongside people and demanded that they live up to its standard (Amos 7:7–9).

He knew that to anger a king was to court death, yet he deliberately set his course toward martyrdom. Martin Luther King, Jr., was unwilling to soften his voice or lessen his opposition to injustice and war although he had a foreboding of approaching death. For my part, I am troubled that I do not live up to my own standards: I am a pacifist. I do not believe in war. Yet I pay my income tax which buys bombs to kill, rather than refuse to pay it and go to jail!

Herod was troubled. When he heard of Jesus' mighty works, he felt sure that this was John whom he had beheaded come back to life. Thus, "Conscience doth make cowards of us all," as Shakespeare puts it.

Herod had been intrigued by John's preaching, eager to hear him and yet unwilling to yield himself to those teachings. His own guilt made him a coward in John's presence. At the banquet in a moment of enthusiasm, perhaps drunk and eager to make an impression on his guests, he made his reckless promise. "Half my kingdom" was a commonplace phrase. When the girl asked for John the Baptist's head, the king was in a dilemma. He liked John. He was also superstitious and feared that to kill John might bring serious consequences. His vanity and his desire to appear strong and magnanimous kept him from breaking his word, much as he wished to.

Herodias smarted under the lash of John's words. To what extremes a grudge and revengeful feelings can take us! She uses her daughter's possibly innocent charms (she seems to have been but a child) and implicates her in this ghastly request for murder.

The girl was unwittingly used. She was a product of the court and accustomed to seeing servants as conveniences, impersonal objects rather than persons. To her John was just a prisoner, not a human being.

Mark's reason for including this story is to recount the growing danger: now John has gone, how long will it be before they close in on Jesus! He is constantly living, as we said above, under the shadow of the cross.

QUESTIONS

How well do you relate to a forthright, aggressive firebrand like John? In some ways Ralph Nader reminds me of John the Baptist. Is there something of the fiery denunciating spirit in you? Do you like to tell people off? To expose their faults? Is it always done with love? Where is the place where obedience to God's will becomes too costly for you, where you fall short of the spirit of martyrdom?

Verse 16: Give an example of where some action of yours has come back to haunt you, as it did in Herod's case. Have you been able to be honest and confess some such incident? Has such honesty robbed it of its power to haunt and hurt you?

Verses 23, 26: Can you think of a promise you made under emotional duress—at a deathbed, in a moment of weakness, or under undue excitement? Would it be right to break such a promise if later events showed that it would work harm to people? What has been your experience?

Verse 19: Herodias nursed and fostered her grudge. What has been your experience with hurt feelings, bitterness and resentment? Have you found a way to get rid of these? Do you tend to nurse them until they explode in anger or find an outlet in some diabolical plot? How do you handle negative feelings? Do you recognize them as soon as they begin to form? Do you immediately talk them over with God? With another person? Do you offer them to God and receive forgiveness and a sense of well-being?

Verses 22–25: Do we exploit others? Showing off our children as extensions of our egos? Talking to and through our children when husband and wife are angry with each other? Sending a child to buy a second article in a store ("one to a customer")? What does all of this do to the child? To you?

John's death emphasized to Jesus that he lived under the threat of death. How do you handle situations like this: Hearing that another died of cancer or other serious illness when you are similarly afflicted? Hearing of unfortunate happenings to other youth when you have teenagers of your own? In other words, are you being called on to live under the shadow of a cross? With what attitude do you face it? With joy? (See Heb. 12:2b.)

9.
REDIRECTING LOVE'S ENERGIES

Mark 6:30–44

(30) The apostles returned to Jesus, and told him all that they had done and taught. (31) And he said to them, "Come away by yourselves to a lonely place, and rest a while." For many were coming and going, and they had no leisure even to eat. (32) And they went away in the boat to a lonely place by themselves. (33) Now many saw them going, and knew them, and they ran there on foot from all the towns, and got there ahead of them. (34) As he landed he saw a great throng, and he had compassion on them, because they were like sheep without a shepherd; and he began to teach them many things. (35) And when it grew late, his disciples came to him and said, "This is a lonely place, and the hour is now late; (36) send them away, to go into the country and villages round about and buy themselves something to eat." (37) But he answered them, "You give them something to eat." And they said to him, "Shall we go and buy two hundred denarii worth of bread, and give it to them to eat?" (38) And he said to them, "How many loaves have you? Go and see." And when they had found out, they said, "Five, and two fish." (39) Then he commanded them all to sit down by companies upon the green grass. (40) So they sat down in groups, by hundreds and by fifties. (41) And taking the five loaves and the two fish he looked up to heaven, and blessed, and broke the loaves,

and gave them to the disciples to set before the people; and he divided the two fish among them all. (42) And they all ate and were satisfied. (43) And they took up twelve baskets full of broken pieces and of the fish. (44) And those who ate the loaves were five thousand men.

Verse 30: The disciples found a listening ear when Jesus returned. A boy returning somewhat late from school was met with, "Hurry now, you'll be late for the dentist." Mother did not say, "How did school go today?" or "You and Bill always have a good time walking home together from school, don't you!" A girl recently returned from a summer conference where, unbeknown to her mother, she had made a commitment of her life to Christ. The first words she heard were, "Thank goodness you are home. I've had to do all the work alone. Start peeling the potatoes for supper." What an art— this art of welcoming the members of our family as they come home!

Verses 31–32: Jesus knew the need for alternation between work and rest, outgo and intake. We see our work in better perspective from a vantage point without. Tired minds and bodies do not function well.

Verse 33: Crowds are often thoughtless. We crowd in on dignitaries. We violate privacy and quietude. Curiosity often causes us to ride roughshod over the personhood and intimacy of others.

Verse 34: Jesus expected a quiet place and found a crowd of people. How easy for him to have been angry, not so much for himself, but for his disciples! They needed rest, time for reflection, and an opportunity to talk over their two-by-two adventures. Jesus must have been tempted to be possessive of them and eager for their welfare. He could well have said angrily, "Can't we have any peace? Isn't there any place where we can be alone?"

His great love for his disciples which was flowing toward them in his plan to have a quiet retreat was abruptly and rudely blocked. How often we set out with loving plans only to have them circumvented by unthinking or even hostile people. The impossibility of carrying out these plans makes us uptight and even resentful.

Love is power. When it is stopped or thwarted it does not just disappear. If not expressed, it turns into negative forces of hostility or bitterness. I may feel warmly toward someone and go to greet him. If he rejects me, my natural reaction is to be critical and resentful. My love has not evaporated into thin air but has changed form, and what was an attitude of warmth is now one of frigidity.

Jesus could have reacted in bitterness against these people, but instead, he redirected this energy of love into other channels. The love was used, but in another way than he originally planned. He viewed the throng, not as intruders or interrupters, but as people to be loved. He had compassion on them and saw them in terms of their needs (lonely, lost "sheep without a shepherd") and not in terms of their sin (their rude interruption of his plans). The love that he intended to give to his disciples in the form of fellowship and teaching, he used in another direction as he began "to teach them many things." Jesus exhibited here a nimbleness and fluidity of spirit where love changed its direction according to the needs of the situation.

Verses 35–38: Jesus tested the resources of his disciples as he asked them to feed these people. They saw only the visible and tangible assets in the treasurer's bag, whereas he used this opportunity to emphasize the power of trust in God. He would lift their standard of measurement from the seen to the unseen, their thoughts from physical food to spiritual food. "Man does not live by bread alone." The mighty work that follows teaches us that Jesus is the Bread of Life and that satisfaction of this hunger is life's greatest priority.

Jesus ascertained that the immediate resources were five loaves and two fish. The disciples saw these as totally inadequate (cf. Andrew in John 6:9, "What are they among so many?") . For Jesus this was the place to begin using unseen resources. God always starts with our little, and as we obey him, it turns into his abundance.

Jesus used this incident to help the disciples see the kind of situation they would face after he had left them. He said, "You give them something to eat." To give people spiritual food will be *their* responsibility after the physical Jesus has left, even as it is the responsibility of the church to feed its people in every age. In the absence of the historical Jesus, God trusts us to distribute the Bread of Life, which is the living Christ.

Verses 39–40: At the close of Jesus' teaching, some of the people, hungry and restless, could well have stood up and started to mill around. Jesus bade them sit down in groups of stated sizes. It is well to have life's situations in hand and to marshal facts and/or people before you where you can more easily deal with them.

Verse 41: Jesus used the Jewish formula with the four verbs *take, bless, break* and *give.* See also the Last Supper (14:22).

Verses 42–44: This story is recorded not that we may be astounded at the multiplication of material food, but that we should believe in Jesus Christ who is the Bread of Life. John's Gospel records what was undoubtedly the teaching of the early church: miracles as such are not important. The signs and mighty works are that we may believe on Jesus Christ and, as John wrote, feed on him, the living Bread, and have Eternal Life (See John 6:26–40).

QUESTIONS

Verse 30: Do people find the "listening ear" when they come to you, as the disciples must have found in Jesus?

Verses 31–32: How wise are you in alternating intake and outgo? Prayer and service? Are you a compulsive thinker and dreamer, or a compulsive worker? What is God's Spirit saying to you about the need to take time off from work to play or rest? Or, if you are the thinker, how about getting into action? What action or what rest is he suggesting? Do you continue to work when over-tired or overexcited? What is God saying about this?

Verse 33: Give an instance where you, like the crowd in the story, intruded on someone who had sought rest and seclusion. What led to this thoughtlessness? How have you changed?

Verse 34: We have asked the question earlier (5:24b–34), "How do you handle interruptions?" Now we ask, "Are you aware of the process by which, when your plans and the flow of your love are abruptly halted, you can redirect these energies?"

Have you found yourself angry when your plans were interrupted, delayed, frustrated? Jesus solved his dilemma by seeing his interrupters as sheep without a shepherd. Can you see those who interrupt you not as people at fault, but people in need?

The further step is to minister to those who block your plans. Give examples where an initial desire to be angry or unresponsive has been redirected toward helping or serving those who caused your frustration. I can remember leaning on my car horn when my wife and children were making me late for an appointment. The thought came to me, "Stop blowing the horn, go in the house and help her with the children and do it with joy." What are some thoughts that God gives to you?

Jesus' plans were not self-centered ones but for the benefit of his disciples. Do you find you are more tempted to be angry when your thwarted plans are for others or for some good cause? Does this make you feel your anger is justified? Talk about this. Give an example where you rechanneled your emotions, and your anger was turned again into love.

Verses 35–38: Do you measure the potential of a situation by the visible resources? If someone suggests a project, is your first reaction, "We don't have that kind of money"? Do you count the cash and then plan your program? Or do you dream God's dreams, think with the largeness of his thoughts, and then move into action? Are you the kind of a person who always says, "Someone around here has to be practical"? This could be right, or it could be that you are limiting God. What do *you* think?

Verses 39–42: As there was abundance of food for the multitude, so today in Jesus the risen and ever-living Lord, there is ample supply of spiritual food for us all. How great are God's resources through Christ! Yet how often we feed on chaff—the world's stories of crime, the gossip of the community. About a week ago I asked myself, "What am I most eager to hear when I awake in the morning?" Three things flashed across my mind in this order. "How the Boston Red Sox did last night, what the weather is going to be, and what my program is for today." I suddenly realized how far down the scale was my eagerness to hear a word of joy and commendation from God and to sense his indwelling and his direction for the day. What are your priorities?

God is saying to us today, as did Jesus then, "Give them something to eat." How do you interpret this command in your situation? Are you limiting what you give because of your human inadequacies of fear and doubt, or are you giving with the resources of God? (See Eph. 3:16.)

10.
TAKE HEART!

(45) Immediately he made his disciples get into the boat and go before him to the other side, to Bethsaida, while he dismissed the crowd. (46) And after he had taken leave of them, he went into the hills to pray. (47) And when evening came, the boat was out on the sea, and he was alone on the land. (48) And he saw that they were distressed in rowing, for the wind was against them. And about the fourth watch of the night he came to them, walking on the sea. He meant to pass by them, (49) but when they saw him walking on the sea they thought it was a ghost, and cried out; (50) for they all saw him, and were terrified. But immediately he spoke to them and said, "Take heart, it is I; have no fear." (51) And he got into the boat with them and the wind ceased. And they were utterly astounded, (52) for they did not understand about the loaves, but their hearts were hardened.

(53) And when they had crossed over, they came to land at Gennesaret, and moored to the shore. (54) And when they got out of the boat, immediately the people recognized him, (55) and ran about the whole neighborhood and began to bring sick people on their pallets to any place where they heard he was. (56) And wherever he came, in villages, cities, or country, they laid the sick in the market places, and besought him that they might touch even the fringe of his garment; and as many as touched it were made well.

Verse 45: It is a fine art both to receive and to dismiss people with grace and affection. *Verse 46:* Mark mentions Jesus' going to pray very casually. It must have been a well-established pattern. Jesus well knew the need for replenishing his spiritual powers.

Verses 47–51: The message in this story is similar to that of Jesus stilling the storm (4:35–41). The church to which this Gospel was directed was undergoing persecution. Jesus was not physically present with these Christians. They were in "distress." But the risen Christ who was ever beside them was a reality (not a "ghost"), one who could enter intimately into their situation (he got into the boat with them), and bring salvation and peace to their hearts.

God's saving grace comes to us at the time we are actually *in* our troubles. "When thou passest through the waters, I will be with thee" (Isa. 43:2, KJV). Even before we call he is already answering (Isa. 65:24). We are called on to sense his presence during the storms of life, not merely when they are over.

Verse 48: He will not force his attention on us. He will not violate our freedom. He awaits our request. "He was going to pass them by" (NEB). I find in myself a stubbornness that prefers to handle matters myself. I sometimes refuse proffered help, wanting to do a thing in my own way. God will not enter our lives until we ask him. The disciples' cry for help was Jesus' passport for entrance. There are times when, in our fright, we fail to recognize that it is God who is approaching. He may be in a sickness that lays us low, in a national depression after war or profligate spending. We may be terrified by the methods of God's approach. But he is for real and comes with help and hope. In these troubled situations, the words of Jesus come to us through the centuries, "Take heart, it is I; have no fear."

Verses 51–52: The disciples were "dumbfounded" (NEB). I, too, find myself amazed at the mighty works of God. I keep telling myself, "Sometime you will get to the place where you will believe in the goodness of God and learn to expect miracles." Yet as new situations approach I find myself with the same lack of faith and am surprised once more by the grace and goodness of God. When will I ever learn to trust him and to expect miracles!

Verses 53–56: Jesus faced here the problems of popularity and success: recognition, thronging crowds, cries for help, little privacy. In the midst of all this he continues to respond to the needs about him. If he felt "virtue" (power) leave him after the healing of one woman, how depleted he must have felt as many touched his cloak! All who touched him were healed.

QUESTIONS

Verse 45: How do you welcome and bid farewell to people? Your own family, your fellow workers, your peers at school? When little children leave for school, do you send them off with nervous warnings and urgings, or with warm affirmation and expressions of confidence and love?

Verse 46: What part does prayer play in your life?

A pietistic habit somewhat lacking in reality and power? A natural regular turning to God for infilling and restoration of faith, power? A desperate measure used in emergency as one uses his fire insurance policies? Talk of this.

Verses 48–49: How do you tend to react in a critical situation when the elements of life (nature or people) seem to be against you? Is your attitude, "Why does this have to happen to me?" "You've forgotten me, God" or "You're here, God, in the middle of this problem with me. What are you trying to teach me? What are you saying to me?" The words, "He meant to pass by them," do not mean that God is not concerned about us, but that he is available awaiting our call. Do you see God as always present but often withholding himself so as to call for initiative and faith on our part?

Verse 50: To what extent have we really appropriated the words, "Take heart, it is I; do not be afraid"? Is religion still a matter of duty, morality, fulfilling compulsively our childhood habit patterns? Or is it a call to courage, to take heart, to brave the storm, to move into difficult situations, into places of need bringing succor, into situations of injustice bringing justice and hope to the oppressed, ever climbing new Calvaries "with a step that turns not back"? Interpret the last question as it relates to specific situations in your present-day life, such as a hospital, a rest home, underpaid workers, drug addicts, parolees, lonely teenagers, civic corruption. Which of these is the particular niche God is asking you to fill?

Verses 51–52: How many miracles must Christ perform before we trust him! Our humanity seems to be such that we will always approach new and difficult situations in "fear and trembling," destined always to be surprised by Christ's presence and power there! Reflect on this.

Verses 53–56: The people recognized Jesus, flocked to him—saying something like, "Here comes that Healer." Does recognition by people trouble you? If you are successful, do their flattery, their insistence, their demands weary you? If you are failing, does their estimate of you limit your activities, fill you with fear and lessen your incentive?

Note how Jesus met and ministered to the crowd. We can well believe that each was an individual to be specially cherished and loved during that moment that he touched person after person.

Amid the busyness of life, and in the midst of people, can you keep quietly attuned to God, carrying on with your task, seeing people as persons and children of God?

11.
TODAY'S TRADITIONS

Mark 7:1–13

(1) Now when the Pharisees gathered together to him, with some of the scribes, who had come from Jerusalem, (2) they saw that some of his disciples ate with hands defiled, that is, unwashed. (3) (For the Pharisees, and all the Jews, do not eat unless they wash their hands, observing the tradition of the elders; (4) and when they come from the market place, they do not eat unless they purify themselves; and there are many other traditions which they observe, the washing of cups and pots and vessels of bronze.) (5) And the Pharisees and the scribes asked him, "Why do your disciples not live according to the tradition of the elders, but eat with hands defiled?" (6) And he said to them, "Well did Isaiah prophesy of you hypocrites, as it is written, 'This people honors me with their lips, but their heart is far from me; (7) in vain do they worship me, teaching as doctrines the precepts of men.' (8) You leave the commandments of God, and hold fast the tradition of men."

(9) And he said to them, "You have a fine way of rejecting the commandment of God, in order to keep your tradition! (10) For Moses said, 'Honor your father and your mother'; and, 'He who speaks evil of father or mother, let him surely die'; (11) but you say, 'If a man tells his father or his mother, What you would have gained from me is Corban' (that is, given to God) —(12) then you no longer permit him to do anything

for his father or mother, (13) thus making void the word of God through your tradition which you hand on. And many such things you do."

Verses 1–5: The disciples had forgotten to wash their hands before eating. (It sounds quite modern: "Johnny, have you washed your hands ready for dinner?") The Pharisees believed themselves to be the custodians of their religion, responsible for its orthodoxy and fidelity to the traditions of the past. Hence their emphasis on laws and customs rather than human values.

Verses 6–8: Jesus was angry and forthright, called them hypocrites, and declared that God's commands were superior to their traditions. *Verses 9–12:* He pointed to a vicious practice they had cultivated. Instead of honoring their parents by taking financial care of them in their older years, they declared their money to be *Corban,* that is, "given to God." It could not then be used for their parents, but it still could be used for themselves. The commandment, "Honor thy father and thy mother," thus had been circumvented. *Verse 13:* God's word was thwarted by their selfish tradition. Thus man seeks to "play God" and even to outwit him.

Man's traditions today tend to separate people and build barriers between them. God's emphasis is on human values. Jesus sought to build community. Man divides community into "insiders" and "outsiders," "old-timers" and "newcomers," "town and gown." After forty-five years in a New England town a man from another area said, "They are just beginning to accept me now." Said a man, "I respond to the denomination that has my flavor." Tradition often deepens our habits of separation. We live in sects and cliques, cultural, ethnic and national groups.

In contrast to this God sees everyone as brothers and sisters one of another. All stand in need. If we would look at our fellows with the eyes of God, we would see all of humankind as members of one great family. We would be quick to recognize the devices we use to divide person from person: the snob appeal, the power plays, the craving for youth and external beauty.

Let us look at some emerging American customs or traditions: The demands of big business and big profits threaten our ecology and our natural resource reserves. Planned obsolescence and rapidly changing fashions of cars, clothes and furniture run counter to God's teaching of stewardship. A father's compulsive work ethic can rob a child of playtime with parents. A penchant for impeccable table manners can make meals funereal rather than a time of rollicking fun. Keeping up with social standards by changing from car to car and moving from house to house can rob a family of the pleasure of simple things and the joy in the love of God they had in their earlier less affluent days.

A political party, a newspaper, or the TV may determine one's thinking and action. Jesus said, "Love your enemies," but the voices of the world say, "Bomb them." The Word says, "God is no respecter of persons," but many people copy the racial prejudices of a TV commentator, or a favorite editor. In countless ways the traditions of men contradict the commandments of God.

Every one of us continually establishes patterns of

living which tend to alienate us from our fellows. These patterns harden into traditions, and we find ourselves as a people bound by our customs, enslaved by the civilization we have built. Depersonalization, alienation, lack of freedom, and hopelessness supplant the joy of being a child of God, living with others in a community of trusting love.

QUESTIONS

Take a generous amount of time and list habit patterns or traditions that are part of your life: childhood or family habits, community attitudes, church prejudices, village or city customs, business practices, consensus thinking, editorial leanings and partisan viewpoints. Read through the material above. Which of these habit patterns or traditions are influencing your life today? Do these traditions bring you closer to God and to your fellows? Do they lead to a more intimate family relationship? Do they lead to reality or fantasy? Are these patterns of life leading to greater inner integrity or to a covert phoniness? Give an example (or examples) of a human tradition in your life that works against the commandment of God and a sense of community. Give an example of a tradition you cherish that helps you fulfill the commandment of God and build community.

What do attitudes or traditions like these say to you: "That kind of thing just isn't done"? "What will the neighbors say?" "Whatever would your grandfather have said about that if he had been alive?" "We never spend money on such items"? "Special holidays should be kept for family celebration"?

Are there habit patterns in your life that keep you from truly loving and caring for other people? From truly caring for black people? Persons of other religions, faiths or political persuasions? Talk of this.

Where have customs built barriers within your family? Father always reads the newspaper after dinner. Mother never changes her beauty shop appointment. Mother always rides in the front seat. We don't play with certain children down the street. Are there customs that cause alienation in your life, in the home, the church?

Talk about national traditions of making war and the command of Jesus to love your enemies. Speak of our ghetto and class segregation and the words of Jesus, "Love your neighbor as yourself."

12.
THE SPRINGS OF THOUGHT

Mark 7:14–23

(14) And he called the people to him again, and said to them, "Hear me, all of you, and understand: (15) there is nothing outside a man which by going into him can defile him; but the things which come out of a man are what defile him." (17) And when he had entered the house, and left the people, his disciples asked him about the parable. (18) And he said to them, "Then are you also without understanding? Do you not see that whatever goes into a man from outside cannot defile him, (19) since it enters, not his heart but his stomach, and so passes on?" (Thus he declared all foods clean.) (20) And he said, "What comes out of a man is what defiles a man. (21) For from within, out of the heart of man, come evil thoughts, fornication, theft, murder, adultery, (22) coveting, wickedness, deceit, licentiousness, envy, slander, pride, foolishness. (23) All these evil things come from within, and they defile a man."

Verses 14–15: In this teaching Jesus was referring to the burdensome laws which forbade a man eating certain foods or eating under various conditions. He was saying, "You are defiled not by what you eat, but by the evil thoughts and plans that rise from your heart."

Frequent bathing, impeccable behavior, correct grooming and beauty treatments—any overemphasis on physical cleansing is fastidious and can easily be a compensation for a sense of spiritual uncleanness. Jesus was saying in effect, "If you are really talking about dirt, then put the emphasis where it belongs . . . not on a little grime on your hands, but on the evil harbored in your hearts." This was a staggering statement in those days of ceremonialism, just as strong as Amos's words, "I hate, I despise your feasts . . . but let justice roll down like waters" (Amos 5:21, 24).

The real pollution of life is that which comes out of a man's thinking and desires. Jesus listed them very specifically. Who of us can claim that such thoughts, if not deeds, have not often been in our hearts?

Verses 17–23: Thoughts often come to me unbidden. This I cannot avoid, *but* I am responsible if I give them lodging. I am further responsible if not only entertaining them, I cherish them, foster them, and even turn them into action. It is this hidden defilement that comes out of man's heart and destroys him, according to Jesus' teaching.

Jesus' list of "evil things" is constituted largely of sins against one's fellow man. Falling into these evils militates against our love for our fellow man. How can we love God whom we have not seen, if we do not love our fellow man whom we have seen? (Cf. 1 John 4:20.) Thoughts of ill-will, envy, lust, dishonesty, slander and even the death wish have come to most of us, from time to time. This only reveals our humanity. I have known what it was to desire another minister's pulpit, a man's wife, or to get the better of a church official in a power-play to outvote his plan. As these thoughts come to mind,

I am learning more quickly to come to God and my fellow man and say, "Here I go again, fighting thoughts and desires I cannot handle. You take them, God, and give me your thoughts, your sense of gratitude and praise." Sometimes just talking it over with God is enough, but often I need to open my heart to God in the presence of a trusted friend. This latter always breaks my inflated pride and then the power of God really flows in.

Jesus was concrete in his list of evil things. But this does not mean that we should seek to eradicate them one at a time and leave the root sin untouched. I have been pulling up some yucca plants that are multiplying and crowding out everything else in our garden. I only pulled up what I could see of the plant, together with three or four inches of root. Within a few weeks green shoots appeared: the yucca was alive and growing again because the main roots were still there.

The root sin in my life is wanting to play God and to have my own way. I want to run my own life, be captain of my soul and of other persons' souls too. The Christian's secret of victorious living is to yield his own will, his very inner being, to God through Christ, so that he no longer lives, but Christ lives in and through him (Gal. 2:20). If the root of our being is altered, the growth of soul will be different. If the springs of thought are pure, the waters of living will be clean.

QUESTIONS

As you look at TV commercials, do you ever find a

temptation to let grooming of yourself, or longing for a luxurious car or furniture become a substitute for inner integrity? If so, talk about it. Have good table manners, gracious food, fine appointments in the home become more important to you than inner graces, spontaneous laughter and the furnishings of the mind? Speak of this.

Do you accept full responsibility for your desires, moods, thoughts and deeds? Do you blame your heredity, the current situation, or others? Describe the difference between fleeting, hovering thoughts and those you entertain. Give an example and tell what you did about it.

Have you been working on sins and trying to clean up your life, rather than getting to the root of all sins—the sin of the prideful self that wants to have its own way, run its own life and play God?

If so, will you consider the need to repudiate the position that you can take care of your life, rid yourself of sins and effect a change? That is God's work. Yours and mine is to yield our total selves to him—even the right to run our own lives or think our own thoughts. I find I need constantly to make a new commitment of myself to him for I am taking myself back again and again and running my own life, and seeking to have my own way. Does this sound familiar to you? Talk about this and about who is running your life.

13.
SPEECH, SEASONED WITH SALTY LOVE!

Mark 7:24–37

(24) And from there he arose and went away to the region of Tyre and Sidon. And he entered a house, and would not have any one know it; yet he could not be hid. (25) But immediately a woman, whose little daughter was possessed by an unclean spirit, heard of him, and came and fell down at his feet. (26) Now the woman was a Greek, a Syrophoenician by birth. And she begged him to cast the demon out of her daughter. (27) And he said to her, "Let the children first be fed, for it is not right to take the children's bread and throw it to the dogs." (28) But she answered him, "Yes, Lord; yet even the dogs under the table eat the children's crumbs." (29) And he said to her, "For this saying you may go your way; the demon has left your daughter." (30) And she went home, and found the child lying in bed, and the demon gone.

(31) Then he returned from the region of Tyre, and went through Sidon to the Sea of Galilee, through the region of the Decapolis. (32) And they brought to him a man who was deaf and had an impediment in his speech; and they besought him to lay his hand upon him. (33) And taking him aside from the multitude privately, he put his fingers into his ears, and he spat and touched his tongue; (34) and looking up to heaven, he sighed, and said to him, "Ephphatha," that is, "Be opened." (35) And his ears were opened, his tongue was

released, and he spoke plainly. (36) And he charged them to tell no one; but the more he charged them, the more zealously they proclaimed it. (37) And they were astonished beyond measure, saying, "He has done all things well; he even makes the deaf hear and the dumb speak."

Verse 24: Jesus was seeking quiet (see 6:31). As many times before, he had to give up the idea of rest and be willing to serve another, and this time a foreigner. *Verses 25–26:* This mother did for her daughter what she probably would not have done for herself.

Jesus was willing to move beyond his ministry to the Jews in the community of Galilee. Mark undoubtedly saw this as an indication and promise that the gospel would be proclaimed to the Gentiles. Jesus is always surprising us, breaking out of small circles of interest and enlarging his sphere of influence. Just so he pushes us out to work in new areas that challenge us.

Verse 27: Jesus demanded of this mother a new degree of humility (her willingness to accept if need be the epithet of "dog"—though he used the diminutive "little dog," meaning a pet) and elicited both her eagerness and faith.

These words of Jesus were out of keeping with his spirit unless we assume that he had a warm whimsical smile as he spoke. He knew the racial barriers and tensions. He implied, "You know that we are not supposed to be talking together like this."

Verse 28: The woman replied in the same spirit: with a smile and yet anxiously. This reply gives evidence of a good self-image. Many of us could easily have felt rebuked and have been crushed by Jesus' words. Instead, she came back with wit and humor. Our response to life is often an indication of our inner sense of security. We grow not by recoiling from confrontation, but by entering into direct and loving dialogue, neither waiting for God's grace with passive submission nor arrogantly claiming our rights.

Jesus had a strong sense of priorities. He dealt with the mother before healing the daughter. Parents can easily be blocks to the healing of their children, radiating fear and pessimism in the home. Callers in a hospital can bring gloom as they commiserate.

Whenever I called at the home of a sick child, I first spent time with the parents if possible. People who love each other are on the same wavelength. When the parents are filled with anxiety, this is unconsciously transmitted to the sick child and hinders recovery. So I seek to lead the parents into a confident faith in order that they may radiate peace and healing rather than fear. Often I would leave the home without even seeing the child, knowing that God's healing would flow through the parents to the child, for now their prayers and attitudes would not be feverish and frightened but those of confident trust.

Verse 29: The faith of Jesus was amazing. Often I have prayed for someone's healing and then said, "Let me know how your boy gets along"! But Jesus commanded and believed that the healing had taken place.

Verses 31–35: Here is another story to show us the mighty working of God through Jesus which demonstrated that he was indeed God's Son, the promised Messiah and the Lord of life.

Jesus brought a dual healing to this deaf-mute. He

would bring a similar healing to us not only physically but in the realm of the spirit too.

Physically, God uses doctors, the caring love of family, friends and nurses. He uses faith and prayer. Many of us can tell of amazing miracles of bodily healing.

Spiritually, God is seeking to heal our deafness to the things of the Spirit. We have ears, but hear not!

He seeks also to loosen our tongues. The church often has an impediment in her speech, speaking God's word with faltering or uncertain voice. A great actor once said to a group of ministers, "We actors speak fiction as though it were truth. You ministers speak the truth as though it were fiction."

Verse 36: Jesus felt that the publishing of his mighty works was premature. He was not ready to announce his Messiahship even to the disciples, much less to people at large. In their enthusiasm they disobeyed him. How often, as newly born Christians, we let our exuberance outrun the wisdom of God.

Verse 37: There was astonishment and praise aplenty. The adoration was focused on the miracle and not channeled into a disciplined obedience of this new Rabbi.

QUESTIONS

Verse 24: Check again your willingness to take interruptions in stride and to turn them into opportunities for joyous service. Have you grown in this? Can you handle interruptions better now?

Verse 25: Jesus, whose mission was originally to Jews, is now ministering to a Gentile. What does this say to you? Are there some old molds to be broken in your life? Some restrictions to be lifted? Can your love be let loose to reach someone you have previously thought to be beyond your caring?

Verse 27: Humor must be gentle, loving, and take into consideration the limitations of the listener. Humor can be used as a cop-out to avoid encounter. It can contain veiled barbs or threats. It can be an attempt to say that which we lack the courage to say in straightforward conversation. I see something of all of these in me. How about you? If so, what do you think God wants you to do about each of them?

Verse 28: When people confront us as Jesus did this woman, are we willing to come back with a firm yet loving response? Are we free of hurt feelings? Speak of how you tend to respond in encounter. Would you have been hurt had you been this woman? Felt rejected? Would you have persisted? Would your attitude have been different if the healing had been for yourself?

Verses 29–30: I confess my lack of faith when, after I have prayed for someone's healing, I inquire later as to how he is doing, at times even doubting. What is your experience here?

Verse 32: We know to whom we can come with our ailments of body and soul. "What a friend we have in Jesus,/All our sins and griefs to bear" (Joseph Scriven). Do you find, like me, that you tend to come to Christ more frequently when you are sick than well? A friend of mine said that God said to her recently, "How come it's my body when you are sick, and that when you are well it belongs to you?"!

Verses 33–34: They asked Jesus to lay his hand on

him. What peace and healing there was in that touch! When someone is sick in your home, do you radiate a quiet peace and assurance? Do you panic and are you full of fear? The touch of your hand can retard or aid healing according to your inner attitude. How do you come into the presence of a sick person? Is fear or peace transmitted? Talk of incidents of this. As the patient, have you felt healing by the mere presence of another person?

Verse 35: Think of ways in which the Master can open the ears of your soul so that you may better hear his commands and be more aware of the needs of others and the cries of the underprivileged. What specific things can you do to improve your ability to hear God speak to you? Introduce a listening time in your devotions? Subscribe to periodicals that present opposite and to you unaccustomed points of view? Stay with this thought awhile. What is God saying to you about how well you hear him?

Think through parallel questions and thoughts about speaking. Do you speak more easily with some people than others? Why is this? Does fear enter in? What does God want you to do about witnessing? Do you speak freely to God, your family, the underprivileged, or people with divergent views from your own? With whom are you too voluble? With whom are you tongue-tied? What has God to say about improving communication with the people in your life?

Verse 36: Forty years ago I had an experience of renewal in Christ that changed the direction of my life. I talked of my new experience most unwisely and inopportunely. I thought everyone should have what I had and I pressured people right and left. Some felt I was arrogant: "You act as if you had something I needed."

Do you recall a time when you unadvisedly blurted out the Good News, and then of a time when you held back—and the results?

Verse 37: The last verse is a paean of praise that I find myself offering to God as I contemplate the work of Christ in me. "Truly," I can say as I look at my life, "he has done all things well." He is teaching me to listen more both to him and others, where once I had been insensitive and deaf. He is teaching me to be timely in speech as well as in silence. Slowly, yet surely, in him I am becoming whole. As I review the goodness of God to me, through Christ, I am, in the words of this verse, "astonished beyond measure."

What is your witness and response to this verse?

14.
WHICH LEAVEN IS AT WORK?

Mark 8:1–21

(1) In those days, when again a great crowd had gathered, and they had nothing to eat, he called his disciples to him, and said to them, (2) "I have compassion on the crowd, because they have been with me now three days, and have nothing to eat; (3) and if I send them away hungry to their homes, they will faint on the way; and some of them have come a long way." (4) And his disciples answered him, "How can one feed these men with bread here in the desert?" (5) And he asked them, "How many loaves have you?" They said, "Seven." (6) And he commanded the crowd to sit down on the ground; and he took the seven loaves, and having given thanks he broke them and gave them to his disciples to set before the people; and they set them before the crowd. (7) And they had a few small fish; and having blessed them, he commanded that these also should be set before them. (8) And they ate, and were satisfied; and they took up the broken pieces left over, seven baskets full. (9) And there were about four thousand people. (10) And he sent them away; and immediately he got into the boat with his disciples, and went to the district of Dalmanutha.

(11) The Pharisees came and began to argue with him, seeking from him a sign from heaven, to test him. (12) And he sighed deeply in his spirit, and said, "Why does this generation seek a sign? Truly, I say to you, no

sign shall be given to this generation." (13) And he left them, and getting into the boat again he departed to the other side.

(14) Now they had forgotten to bring bread; and they had only one loaf with them in the boat. (15) And he cautioned them, saying, "Take heed, beware of the leaven of the Pharisees and the leaven of Herod." (16) And they discussed it with one another, saying, "We have no bread." (17) And being aware of it, Jesus said to them, "Why do you discuss the fact that you have no bread? Do you not yet perceive or understand? Are your hearts hardened? (18) Having eyes do you not see, and having ears do you not hear? And do you not remember? (19) When I broke the five loaves for the five thousand, how many baskets full of broken pieces did you take up?" They said to him, "Twelve." (20) "And the seven for the four thousand, how many baskets full of broken pieces did you take up?" And they said to him, "Seven." (21) And he said to them, "Do you not yet understand?"

Verses 1–10: These verses suggest thoughts similar to those we had when reading of the feeding of the five thousand (6:35–44): namely, that the story is told in order that we may know that Jesus as the Son of God is the Bread of Life; that it would be the responsibility of the disciples after Jesus left to feed people with the Living Bread, Jesus Christ; that the continuing responsibility of the church through the centuries and of us Christians today is to share with others this Christ, the Bread of Life.

Verse 11: The Pharisees wanted a sign that would speak to them on their terms. They demanded to be satisfied in a spectacular way. They would not accept the evidence of the miracles of healing already performed, nor recognize the strong caring personhood of this man. God demonstrated through Jesus (in mighty works such as the feeding of the multitude) that he has unlimited power which he freely shares with us in Christ through his grace. In our insensitivity we fail to recognize this and say, "God, give us a sign." With the ever-present Christ within, we need no sign. *Verse 12:* Jesus refused to provide the sign, for to give it would not convince them. There was no desire on their part to be convinced. Luke's parable of the rich man and Lazarus ends with Abraham saying, "Neither will they be convinced if some one should rise from the dead" (Luke 16:31).

If we are going to appreciate anyone and learn from him, we have to listen to him in terms of his own idiom and frame of reference. The Pharisees wanted Jesus to meet *their* demands with a sign that would fit into *their* concept of a miracle. They would not listen to Jesus as God's Messiah and a harbinger of the new Kingdom of God.

When I speak with a man who has a different theological viewpoint than mine or who has a different approach to the Bible, I cannot truly hear him if I quarrel with his theology or biblicism. If I let religious doctrines or points of view turn me off, I am not communicating with him. If I set him free to speak and believe as he will, if I seek to get behind his words and sympathetically listen to what he is actually saying, then I begin to hear him. Each man should be heard in his own idiom, even as any national can best be comprehended if he is listened to in his native language.

Verses 14–17: How easily we think on a material level, when God seeks to raise our sights to the spiritual. A group of people were contemplating erecting a new and larger church building. Looking at the beautiful architect's drawings one man remarked, "We just don't have what it would take to put up a building like that." Everyone present interpreted his words to refer to their lack of money, yet what he really referred to was their lack of faith.

Verses 18–21: Jesus challenged his disciples to live in a world of faith. Here the enemies are not so much the lack of material goods as the corroding influence of legalism—the leaven of the Pharisees—and the inroads of cynicism and worldliness—the leaven of Herod. Jesus proclaimed that life constantly calls for faith to believe in the seemingly impossible, and that the visible often belies what faith would affirm.

QUESTIONS

Verse 2: Jewish hospitality is proverbial, and Jesus illustrated it in this incident. Can you recall an example of compassion on your part when the demands on your love were prolonged?

Verse 4: Do you ever find yourself saying, "How can we undertake this project with so little money?" ". . . with so few people?" "We've never before faced this kind of a situation"? In Christ, the power we already possess is multiplied and released to face new and difficult situations.

Verse 15: The "leaven of the Pharisees" occurs when

persons have a strong sense of rectitude and believe that they have the whole truth neatly wrapped up in their package of thinking. Do you see God's Spirit nudging you out into new situations that call for growth with its painful processes of discovery, possible failure, and need for new faith? Tell of an instance of God pushing you out into a new situation where you were challenged either to grow and risk hurt, or to retreat and feel secure.

Think about your willingness to listen to someone who speaks in a different idiom or frame of reference. For instance, is it harder for you to be comfortable with someone who is holding in his hands a glass of beer? With a man who constantly argues? Who repeatedly "throws" Bible verses at you? Who curses? Or announces he is an atheist? To whom do you find it most difficult to listen? With whom is it difficult to empathize? Be specific in this and see what God would have you do about such attitudes.

The "leaven of Herod" occurs as persons become cynical and say, "All men have a price." "Corruption is in every part of government." "Money and power are all that people believe in these days." Do you find yourself believing this? Is there a need for you to grow in this area?

Speak of the contrast between the leaven of the Pharisees, of Herod, and that of Jesus Christ. Tell of occasions when you have seen each of them at work in your life. Leaven may be thought of as meaning "quietly working power" or "teaching" or both.

Verses 17–18: How severely Jesus spoke to the disciples in verses 17b, 18 and 21. In what parallel way is he speaking to you today? I find that I run scared before nearly every retreat or conference that I lead. Often I doubt that miracles will happen. But they always do! I need to believe that this mighty power of God through Christ is always available to me. My heart is often "hardened," that is, insensitive to the fact that the grace and power of God are available to me in every situation. Speak of similar instances in your life.

15.
TOUCH ME

Mark 8:22–26

(22) And they came to Bethsaida. And some people brought to him a blind man, and begged him to touch him. (23) And he took the blind man by the hand, and led him out of the village; and when he had spit on his eyes and laid his hands upon him, he asked him, "Do you see anything?" (24) And he looked up and said, "I see men; but they look like trees, walking." (25) Then again he laid his hands upon his eyes; and he looked intently and was restored, and saw everything clearly. (26) And he sent him away to his home, saying, "Do not even enter the village."

Three times within these five verses we are told that Jesus touched the blind man. There are people who feel uncomfortable with touching or being touched. For years I longed for physical contacts but felt shy and uncertain about making advances. The Spirit of Christ is gradually setting me free to love with both heart and hand. My body should be the extension of my inner self, where there is a deep love that longs for expression.

There is a sense in which the physical touch completes and fulfills the decision to love. Many of the people Jesus touched must have been repulsive. Merely to smile and speak to them would have short-changed the recipient, and would have failed to complete the act of outgoing love on Jesus' part. I recall Danny Kaye, when telling about the work of UNICEF, would take little emaciated and diseased children and cuddle them in his arms.

There needs to be discipline in any use of physical touch. Touch can express anger and result in harm such as cruelly punishing a child; on the other hand, touch could turn to a possessive or unwise and amorous demonstration.

A deacon called frequently on a sick fellow parishioner. After his death, he called to comfort the young widow. All this was probably done in good faith and Christian love, but indiscipline entered in. The calls on the widow became more frequent and the result was that he left his wife and four children, secured a divorce and eventually married the young widow.

We know deep within ourselves when our touch is in genuine Christian love, or if it is becoming something to be selfishly and sensuously enjoyed. Recently I was finishing a strenuous week in a church where I was being entertained at the parsonage. The three of us, the pastor, his wife and I, sat snacking at the table after the concluding service. I told them of my spiritual emptiness, my fatigue, the likelihood of temptation when I was exhausted, and of my longing to be home with my wife. We all prayed specifically for my infilling and strengthening. The prayer concluded, the pastor gave me a great bear hug and his wife added her hug and an affectionate kiss. While going to sleep my thoughts dwelt awhile on that kiss and, waking in the night, I thought of it again.

At the breakfast table, I told my friends what had happened and added, "I want, and I need your love very much. I felt last night as each of you embraced me that you mediated the love of Jesus to me. It was God, in the flesh, touching me. I was strengthened and blessed. However, both in giving and receiving love I must be controlled and disciplined." Whenever I begin to recall a kiss or an embrace and enjoy it in memory and separate it from the total experience, then I am prostituting something beautiful which was given to me in order to receive the love of God through one of his children.

To be free to touch is to open the door to the use of great power—for love is power. It is far better to wrestle with temptation and to have to discipline ourselves, than to stifle our emotions and not give expression to our deeper selves.

This miracle of healing is another evidence of God's mighty power through Jesus. He constantly gave evidence of a God who is always working for total wholeness. The love of God in the heart of Jesus and the faith that God would use him to bless and heal lay at the center of these miracles. You and I may claim God's love and faith also and in Christ's Spirit seek to bring his healing to others. The fact that Jesus needed to touch the man twice could suggest that this was a severe case, or that we need to persevere in our faith and love as we bring Christ's healing to people.

QUESTIONS

Do you tend to be uncomfortable touching or being

touched? Is it easier to touch a little child or a baby than an adult? Why is this? Do you feel threatened with an adult? Afraid of being rejected? Afraid of being misunderstood? Going too far? Think through the use of your hands in the light of how frequently Jesus touched. What is God saying to you? Think through the use of your body—given in daily toil, given in service to the family, given in sexual relations, in eating and drinking. Is your body offered in ministry to the needs of others? Is your body given in service for the "joy that is set before you" (see Heb. 12:2)?

When Christ sets free his love within you, do you let it flow through you, not only in words and acts, but also in touch? Speak of places where one can be undisciplined in touch: trying to embrace a resisting teenager; unloving punishment; picking up a little tot every time he falls; indulging in a fishlike handshake; a too sexy embrace; embracing so frequently that it loses its deeper meaning.

Do you think of yourself as a channel of healing? A mother cuddles and rocks a frightened child, believing that in so doing healing and peace pass into the child. Describe some appropriate and meaningful ways in which both by words, touch and body language you can minister to and help heal youth, adults, and also various members of your family. Think of specific situations.

Have you laid your hands on people and specifically prayed for another's healing? Speak of this. You may have the gift of healing. You will never know until you venture out and try.

16.
"YOU ARE THE CHRIST"

Mark 8:27–9:1

(27) And Jesus went on with his disciples, to the villages of Caesarea Philippi; and on the way he asked his disciples, "Who do men say that I am?" (28) And they told him, "John the Baptist; and others say, Elijah; and others one of the prophets." (29) And he asked them, "But who do you say that I am?" Peter answered him, "You are the Christ." (30) And he charged them to tell no one about him.

(31) And he began to teach them that the Son of man must suffer many things, and be rejected by the elders and the chief priests and the scribes, and be killed, and after three days rise again. (32) And he said this plainly. And Peter took him, and began to rebuke him. (33) But turning and seeing his disciples, he rebuked Peter, and said, "Get behind me, Satan! For you are not on the side of God, but of men."

(34) And he called to him the multitude with his disciples, and said to them, "If any man would come after me, let him deny himself and take up his cross and follow me. (35) For whoever would save his life will lose it; and whoever loses his life for my sake and the gospel's will save it. (36) For what does it profit a man, to gain the whole world and forfeit his life? (37) For what can a man give in return for his life? (38) For whoever is ashamed of me and of my words in this adulter-

ous and sinful generation, of him will the Son of man also be ashamed, when he comes in the glory of his Father with the holy angels." (1) And he said to them, "Truly, I say to you, there are some standing here who will not taste death before they see the kingdom of God come with power."

Let us first think together of the development of Jesus' sense of mission and its relation to the Messianic dreams of his day. Then let us trace parallels in our own lives and our relation to the American dream in the contemporary scene.

Three stages of growth had marked Jesus' inner life. First, the consciousness of a sense of personal identity, a calling of God that probably came to him as a growing boy deepening as he grew older and walked the hills near Nazareth. Second, the awareness that he was called to be the Messiah, a sense of definite mission. This likely developed gradually in his late teens and twenties, and was perhaps realized at his baptism. Third, the decision as to what kind of a Messiah he would be—the priorities, strategies and goals for his Messiahship. There must have been wrestlings before his baptism, but he won a preliminary victory during the forty days of temptation in the wilderness, a victory which needed to be won again and again as in Caesarea Philippi and Gethsemane.

We can trace these same three stages of growth in ourselves. They may not necessarily take place in sequence, but with interaction and alternation. First, each is called to a sense of his own identity. We are God's children, greatly loved of him and very special to him. We are men and women for whom Jesus Christ died. We are sons and daughters of God, joint heirs with Christ.

Second, we feel a sense of mission and purpose in life. God chooses us, whether dentist or salesman, student or homemaker, lays his hand upon us, and sends us out into this world (John 15:1b; Josh. 1:1–9).

Third, we have to choose what kind of a life style we will live out in this mission of ours. Today the American Dream for many is to make money, live in suburbia, gain promotions, retire early and live in comfort. As Jesus sought in his day to change the Messianic dream from one of self-aggrandizement to that of the Suffering Servant, our task in America is to help our country exemplify the Spirit of this Jesus, the Servant of all. Each of us, whatever his craft or calling, is asked by God to live out this Spirit of Christ in whatever sphere of activity he may live.

Jesus had to choose between aspiring to be a king making all nations subject to him and the lonely ideal of the Suffering Servant as pictured in Isaiah (chap. 53). He went counter to popular sentiment and clamor and chose to establish a Kingdom of love for which he laid down his life. Jesus' opposition to the current national dreams of his countrymen forces us to think through our attitudes toward the direction of our present culture. Are we willing so to live that we counter our contemporary lust for power and profit with the Servant motif of the Master?

Verse 27: Jesus asks this question possibly to assess what people thought of him, but more likely to lead up to the question of what the disciples thought.

Jesus knew what he thought of himself. He had a good self-image. He knew he was God's Son and Messiah.

It is possible that this question could have expressed the doubts that must have entered Jesus' mind at times: "Am I really going to get this new concept of the Messiah through to my disciples? If the leaders kill me, will they kill the dream, too? Will they all revert to the blood-thirsty, power-hungry expectations of a Messianic Rule?"

Verse 29: He turned to his disciples with "Who do you say that I am?" His question implied also, "Are you with me in my mission? Are you sold on my way of life?" Jesus was walking a lonely road. He sought to live out God's way of life among a people who thrived on animosities. He believed in forgiveness and love, not retaliation and hate. He longed for confirmation of his life style from man as well as from God. He longed for human companionship on this solitary trail.

Peter made the reply to Jesus' question. Sometimes his impulsive words brought gladness, at other times sadness to the heart of the Master! This was a time of sincere admiration as he said, "You are the Christ." These words are tantamount to "I believe in you. I want you as my Leader and Messiah." Peter loved Jesus with his heart, but he did not comprehend in his mind Jesus' concept of the Messiah. *Verse 30:* Jesus asks his disciples not to broadcast his Messiahship. People would interpret it in terms of narrow nationalism—a physically powerful kingship. This would militate against his plan to bring new content to the word *Messiah.*

Verses 31–32: When Jesus spelled out his concept of the Messiah, Peter rebuked him, for he was still a Jew at heart clinging to the old idea of an all-powerful monarch ruling over the nations. He liked this loving, caring Rabbi, but when Jesus detailed the cost—"suffer . . . be rejected . . . be killed"—Peter could not go along with it.

Verse 33: Jesus had to rebuke Peter roundly when he found it difficult to accept the fact there might be a rejection of the Messiah.

Verses 34–37: Jesus details what is implied in the previous verses. He enunciates this paradoxical principle of losing to gain, and that one's inner life is of more value than all the world.

Verse 38 is not to be thought of as Christ requiting us for our cowardice, but rather the working out of a fundamental principle of life—if we are ashamed of the truth, then truth will ultimately rise to shame us.

Verse 1 (chap. 9): Jesus and Paul both seem to have expected the "Second Coming" during their lifetimes. This was also the general belief in the church during the first century, but it faded as the years passed by. This expectation has been revived from time to time and in recent years is very strong. Some of us believe that we are not so much at the end of an era that will usher in the Second Coming of Christ, but at the beginning of an era when Christ's Spirit is breaking out anew among us. The Second Coming is in God's hands, and none of us know the hour.

QUESTIONS

Trace the three stages of growth in your life. When

and how has the truth been revealed to you that you are God's child and that he has a special love for you? If this has not happened, will you let it take place as you read these words? God offers you his love freely. He is passionately fond of you.

Second, do you feel a call to your position in life? To your job? Your place in your home? Community? God enters into each situation to make it his plan for you. As you accept it, he will bless you in it, leading you to other situations if that is his will.

Third, what motivates you in your calling—parenthood, childhood, job? Since it is human to advance our own interests, we need to ask ourselves, "Is our motivation self-serving? Power- and success-oriented? Or are we motivated toward others, living lives that joyously spend and give of themselves?" In other words is our attitude akin to the old Messianic spirit or the new one of the Servant that we see in Jesus?

What do you see as the American Dream? Security? Success? Freedom? Maintaining the strongest army? The most powerful atomic weapons? The biggest gross national product? More TVs, planes and food than any other nation? What do you think is God's dream for America? Is it to become a sharing, caring, sacrificing nation, even dying that other nations may live? Is the Jesus way of life as realistic for nations as for individual persons?

Speak of some expressions of the American way of life: "My country first." "My country right or wrong." "Get to the top of the class." "What will the neighbors think?" "Make a good impression." Big money, big house, big success, luxury, comfort, power, dog-eat-dog. Wherein has the American way of life entered into or modified your life style? Do you feel called so to live in the Spirit of Jesus as to seek to modify the American style of life, as leaven or salt, in your church, your community or business? Talk of this.

Now let us consider some individual verses:

Verses 27–29: Have you ever asked anyone to assess your life? With what results? This openness of others can be both helpful and harmful. Jesus accepted Peter's announcement that he was the Messiah but not Peter's interpretation of the life style of the Messiah. Do you have a strong enough self-image carefully to listen to people's estimate of you and your work, and speak out strongly from your own knowledge of your identity? Some of us need to listen more to others, some less. What is your need here?

Verse 31: Have we really grasped the idea that there is a cross at the heart of Christian living? Is not this the very thing that Peter would not or could not see? Have we a willingness to pour out our lives for others? Have we grasped the truth that such a pouring out and dying, under God, becomes "resurrection" both here, and hereafter? God takes our experiences of the cross and turns them into victory.

Verses 32–33: Note the steadfast, tough love of Jesus that stayed with Peter, teaching, training, rebuking, yet always believing in him. Do you stay by people? Or give up too easily? Give some examples of where you are doing this, or failing to do it.

Verses 34–37: Trace the idea of saving and losing life

through some of your areas of living. Has the joy of study and learning lessened when you have worked chiefly to get high marks and honors? Has the joy of the job lessened as you have concentrated on earning more money and advanced rating? Has the simple zest for living lessened as you have sought the more sophisticated luxuries of life? Is the reverse true? Tell of times of the joy of study when it was not for marks, but just for the fun of it. Tell of the shift from mostly desiring increased pay and promotion to a deeper consideration and love of your fellow workers. Tell of ceasing to pull rank, use pressure and to have your own way in the home and the new spirit and joy that have followed. Tell of living more simply and "enjoying it more."

This section of Scripture is pivotal in the Gospel of Mark. We should not leave its study without feeling a renewed dedication both to the Master as our Christ and Messiah and to his life style. I find myself saying, "Yes, Jesus, you are the Christ, God's Word and Life given to me. I believe in you and your life style. You are mine and I am forever yours. I want to invest my life in your service, regardless of the cost." This should be a time of decision. The choice is yours.

17.
EASTER FAITH

Mark 9:2–13

(2) And after six days Jesus took with him Peter and James and John, and led them up a high mountain apart by themselves; and he was transfigured before them, (3) and his garments became glistening, intensely white, as no fuller on earth could bleach them. (4) And there appeared to them Elijah with Moses; and they were talking to Jesus. (5) And Peter said to Jesus, "Master, it is well that we are here; let us make three booths, one for you and one for Moses and one for Elijah." (6) For he did not know what to say, for they were exceedingly afraid. (7) And a cloud overshadowed them, and a voice came out of the cloud, "This is my beloved Son; listen to him." (8) And suddenly looking around they no longer saw any one with them but Jesus only.

(9) And as they were coming down the mountain, he charged them to tell no one what they had seen, until the Son of man should have risen from the dead. (10) So they kept the matter to themselves, questioning what the rising from the dead meant. (11) And they asked him, "Why do the scribes say that first Elijah must come?" (12) And he said to them, "Elijah does come first to restore all things; and how is it written of the Son of man, that he should suffer many things and be treated with contempt? (13) But I tell you that Elijah has come, and they did to him whatever they pleased, as it is written of him."

Verses 2–3: Religious experience records many times when men have witnessed the majesty and mystery of the Divine. God is always revealing himself. Moses saw God in the burning bush (Exod. 3). Isaiah saw him "high and lifted up" in the temple (Isa. 6). Peter, James and John saw the transfigured Jesus on the mountain.

Verse 4: From early boyhood Jesus must have reveled in the stories of the Old Testament, particularly those of Moses and Elijah. In this high moment of spiritual ecstasy and communion, these two stalwart giants leaped out of the pages of history and became real for Jesus. Moses and Elijah represent the law and the prophet. Jesus fulfills both and towers above them with his life of sacrificial love and grace. God revealed himself to and through Jesus, showing us that Jesus was indeed his Son, the living Lord. Thus God affirmed what Peter had said at Caesarea.

Verse 5: Peter wished to hold onto the intimate experience. We all tend to possess and even exploit the glorious moment and hug it to ourselves. Ecstasy best serves its purpose when translated into creative living. The architect's dream needs to be turned into steel and concrete. The biblical vision is to be lived out in love in the family and daily task.

Moments of great spiritual experience generally engender fear. The shepherds were afraid when the angels spoke of Christ's coming. The women and disciples were afraid when told that Jesus had risen. The day of my ordination was filled with fear and awe as I recognized the challenge of the ministry and the greatness of the God who had called me to it. *Verse 6:* Times like these are best served by reverence and silence. Silence was not Peter's long suit. How often we blunder with words and awkwardly break a meaningful mood.

Verse 7: Only a few days before this, Jesus had told his disciples that the style of his Messiahship was to be that of a "suffering servant." This meant that he "must suffer many things, and be rejected . . . and be killed" (8:31). Now God affirms and strengthens his Son through the presence of Moses and Elijah as well as his strong words of affirmation. God is appearing also to the disciples saying in effect, "I want you to listen to my Son. He is the Messiah. His life style is according to my will. Listen to him and follow him." *Verse 8:* The vision was over. The mystical presence had gone. It would be easy to want to recapture the experience and to recall it in sentimental reverie. But visions and mountaintop experiences are to be prelude to action. *Verse 9:* Jesus asked the disciples to keep the incident secret as he did after Peter's declaration at Caesarea Philippi (8:30). They questioned the "rising from the dead" because it was inconceivable that death should ever come to Jesus. For a Messiah to suffer, much less to die, was unthinkable. They could not break away from the centuries-old conception of the Messiah being a king ruling in power and security.

Verse 10: It might have been better had they spoken of their questions to Jesus. He was a forthright man and spoke frankly about people's inner thoughts as when the scribes were questioning Jesus' right to forgive sins (2:8). He would have welcomed their forthrightness. No wonder they questioned! They had not encountered the risen Christ. They did not have an Easter faith, as did Jesus.

Verses 12–13: The Jews thought that Elijah's return would precede the coming of God to judge the world. Some people believed Elijah had come in the form of John the Baptist. John the Baptist was killed. Elijah too was persecuted. Jesus faced the fact that his predecessors suffered and some were killed. Jesus moved steadily forward, knowing that death awaited him. But in his heart was this Easter faith.

QUESTIONS

Verses 2–4: God reveals himself to different people in various ways. Some have mystic experiences with visions and voices. Others have the quiet assurance of being surrounded by God's love—like a little puppy tucked in God's overcoat pocket with his head sticking out! Mine is apt to be in the quieter vein, with a sense of well-being. In what ways does God reveal himself to you? What happens? What are the results? Do they result in a change in your relationships to others or to yourself?

I recall listening to an orchestra play a tone poem in which two themes, representing Good and Evil, vied long and hard for ascendancy, the orchestra ending in a unified paean of victory. It came at a time in my life when I was sorely beset by moods of self-doubt, lustful desires and inordinate ambition. The experience of hearing this music was twofold: It assured me of God's presence with me in my struggle. It inspired me into becoming a changed and new man. Recall an experience when Christ became very real to you. Did you feel affirmed? Strengthened? Did a new life style result?

Verse 5: Give an example when you wanted to cling to a beautiful experience, hoping it would continue rather than getting on with the business of living. To this day I am sometimes reluctant to leave a beautiful passage of Scripture to unscrew the top of a jar of jam for my wife! Speak of the selfishness of indulging in and holding on to rapturous experiences. *Verse 6:* Do you know when to be silent? When to worship silently in awe?

Verse 7: Has God assured you of the Saviorhood and Lordship of Jesus and said authoritatively to you, "Listen to him"? There is a dual affirmation here: God is affirming Jesus as his Son and Messiah. He is also affirming Jesus in the presence of his disciples so that they may believe in him as the Messiah and listen to him. In like manner God would affirm you. Are you letting him tell you that you are his child? Are you letting him love you? Assure you how important you are to him? God through Christ is also seeking to affirm you in the presence of others. Do you feel his affirmation of your calling, your place in the home, at school, on the job, your task in church or community? Do you hear God saying to others about you, "_____, (Insert your name here) is important to me. I love him/her. I want you also to affirm him and listen to him. My love is flowing through him"?

Verse 8: Have you experienced an aloneness or solitariness when a high spiritual moment has passed? Have your friends been quite indifferent about what has been going on within you? How do you react to this?

Verse 9: Are we equally aware of God's commands to be silent as we are of his commands to speak?

Verse 10: Speak of your "Easter faith." Has the Christ really risen for you and is he living in your life? *Verse 12:* Have you thoroughly accepted the truth that while the Christian way is one of joy and adventure, it is also a way of suffering, often with much trouble and persecution? It is reassuring to know that in spite of all that may befall us, the strength of the living Christ never fails. We can trust his promise, "Lo, I am with you alway, even unto the end of the world" (Matt. 28:20, KJV).

18.
LORD, INCREASE OUR FAITH

Mark 9:14–29

(14) And when they came to the disciples, they saw a great crowd about them, and scribes arguing with them. (15) And immediately all the crowd, when they saw him, were greatly amazed, and ran up to him and greeted him. (16) And he asked them, "What are you discussing with them?" (17) And one of the crowd answered him, "Teacher, I brought my son to you, for he has a dumb spirit; (18) and wherever it seizes him, it dashes him down; and he foams and grinds his teeth and becomes rigid; and I asked your disciples to cast it out, and they were not able." (19) And he answered them, "O faithless generation, how long am I to be with you? How long am I to bear with you? Bring him to me." (20) And they brought the boy to him; and when the spirit saw him, immediately it convulsed the boy, and he fell on the ground and rolled about, foaming at the mouth. (21) And Jesus asked his father, "How long has he had this?" And he said, "From childhood. (22) And it has often cast him into the fire and into the water, to destroy him; but if you can do anything, have pity on us and help us." (23) And Jesus said to him, "If you can! All things are possible to him who believes." (24) Immediately the father of the child cried out and said, "I believe; help my unbelief!" (25) And when Jesus saw that a crowd came running together, he rebuked the unclean spirit, saying to it, "You dumb and

deaf spirit, I command you, come out of him, and never enter him again." (26) And after crying out and convulsing him terribly, it came out, and the boy was like a corpse; so that most of them said, "He is dead." (27) But Jesus took him by the hand and lifted him up, and he arose. (28) And when he had entered the house, his disciples asked him privately, "Why could we not cast it out?" (29) And he said to them, "This kind cannot be driven out by anything but prayer."

Verses 16–18: What a contrast between the majestic solitude of the mountain and this scene in the valley: the milling crowd, the helpless nine disciples, a distraught father and son! The forthright Jesus wades right in with "What are you discussing . . . ?" The father correctly describes the symptoms of epilepsy.

Verse 19: Jesus is angry with his disciples, upbraiding them for lack of faith, for slowness of learning, adding, "How long must I endure you?" (NEB). But as in the case of the healing of the man with the withered hand and also the teaching and feeding the multitude he sublimated his anger into service (3:5 and 6:31–34).

Verses 21–23: The boy's condition is chronic, but Jesus says, "All things are possible to him who believes." As with the Syrophoenician mother (7:24–30) Jesus seeks to develop faith in the parent first. Goodspeed translates Jesus' words as "Everything is possible for the one who believes."

Verse 24: The father's reply is, "I have faith, . . . help me where faith falls short" (NEB). With the passing of years I am increasingly amazed at the way in which God honors faith. I have gone into churches and retreat

situations in fear and trembling and yet in faith, claiming God's power—and what miracles have happened!
My faith grew as I went forward and God worked as I
obeyed.

Verse 25: The strength of Jesus which a few minutes
earlier was shown as anger toward his disciples, now
shows itself in sternly rebuking the unclean spirit. We
see Jesus as victor in both the physical and the spiritual
realms.

Verse 26: When physical maladies and the effects of
our particular culture and childhood are deeply seated
in our habit patterns, there is often a drastic struggle as
the shackles of the past are thrown off and a new way of
life embraced. On the Damascus road, Paul fell to the
ground and was blinded. A friend of mine shook and
trembled violently as she faced a childhood traumatic
experience and yielded herself to the love of Jesus and
was healed.

Verses 28–29: "Why could we not cast it out?" I have
asked that question as I have stood in the presence of
evil. I look at the estrangement between the generations.
I see the irrelevance and impotence of many churches.
I see defeated ministers, disintegrating homes, youth
drifting in meaningless boredom. Why can't I do more?
I have to take Jesus' words deeply to myself, "Lee, you
need to spend more time in prayer, my son. Evil cannot
be driven out by anything but prayer."

QUESTIONS

What kind of a picture of Jesus do you form as you

read this story? He loved sinners, he associated with the
sick and needy people, he got angry. He severely rep-
rimanded the disciples he loved. He fearlessly rebuked
and drove out evil spirits. With tenderness he took hold
of a boy's hand. Are you bringing an adult mind to this
study of Jesus, leaving behind childish images and any
feeling that he was a "sweet, precious, unearthly" being?
Do you see him as a warm, vigorous human being with
feelings like your own?

Do you face evil in others, whether physical or spiritual, with strong courage? Jesus faced evil head-on. I am
afraid I tend to evade encounter where I can. Will you
seek to believe with me that the Spirit of Christ in us
desires to flow through you and me so that we can be
used to be victorious over evil of mind and body in ourselves and in others? What steps towards this do you feel
God is asking you to take?

Do you always control your anger? I find it hard to be
angry. As a boy I was taught, "Good boys don't lose their
tempers." So I kept my anger inside and paid for it with
nervous breakdowns. Discuss the right use of anger, the
forthright word, the sharp rebuke, and the sublimation
of anger into constructive channels of loving service.
When my wife punished our young children, she would
always hold them in her arms afterward, as they sobbed
together. I punished them, but could never hold them
afterward. My anger controlled me and the Spirit of the
Master did not. What place does anger have in your life?
Discuss its cleansing and release. Speak of the place of
the healing love that should follow anger.

Sometimes I have felt these stern words of Jesus directed to me: "Lee, how long am I to bear with you?"

I am no longer young, yet I still am needing to learn over and over the same lessons about Christ-centered living. I am often conscious of his angry rebuke of me, yet I never feel that he has given up on me or stopped loving me. On the contrary, he continues to guide, encourage and affirm me. So it is that we grow in Christ. Speak of times when the Master has rebuked you and dealt sternly with you.

Have you ever said, as did the lad's father, "I have faith, . . . help me where faith falls short" (NEB)? What happened? Did you persist in making your request? Was it granted? In our weakness we offer him our will to believe, our desire to have faith. He turns our desire into real faith. Have you tried this? Faith is God's gift, not the product of will power.

19.
MARKS OF DISCIPLESHIP

Mark 9:30–41

(30) They went on from there and passed through Galilee. And he would not have any one know it; (31) for he was teaching his disciples, saying to them, "The Son of man will be delivered into the hands of men, and they will kill him; and when he is killed, after three days he will rise." (32) But they did not understand the saying, and they were afraid to ask him.

(33) And they came to Capernaum; and when he was in the house he asked them, "What were you discussing on the way?" (34) But they were silent; for on the way they had discussed with one another who was the greatest. (35) And he sat down and called the twelve; and he said to them, "If any one would be first, he must be last of all and servant of all." (36) And he took a child, and put him in the midst of them; and taking him in his arms, he said to them, (37) "Whoever receives one such child in my name receives me; and whoever receives me, receives not me but him who sent me."

(38) John said to him, "Teacher, we saw a man casting out demons in your name, and we forbade him, because he was not following us." (39) But Jesus said, "Do not forbid him; for no one who does a mighty work in my name will be able soon after to speak evil of me. (40) For he that is not against us is for us. (41) For truly, I say to you, whoever gives you a cup of water

to drink because you bear the name of Christ, will by no means lose his reward."

Verses 30–32: Jesus sought to be alone with his disciples, in order to have an opportunity to teach them. He set a high priority on the instruction of these twelve men. He was preparing them to be on their own. Jesus repeated to his disciples what he had recently told them: He will be killed and after three days rise again. They cannot comprehend these words (see v. 10). The world says, "Live by living." Jesus said, "Live by dying." The world says, "Do your own thing and be happy." Jesus' words were, "Deny yourself and know my joy." No wonder they did not understand. It was a new concept of living for them. It was a life style contrary to the accepted standards of the world in which they lived then and in which we live now. Two thousand years have brought little change in this regard. The world still believes in the use of force, pressures, intimidation, bombs and bullets. The beatitudes (Matt. 5:3–12) describe a way of life that is totally foreign to the way of life of our contemporary world.

Verses 33–34: The reason they were "completely mystified" (Phillips) by Jesus' words becomes apparent. There was a power struggle going on among them. Each one wanted to be "king of the mountain." Their way of life still savored of that of the world rather than what Jesus was teaching. We only *understand* words when we "stand under" them, when we relate ourselves to their meaning. The disciples were not trying to "die," but to assert their egos, each desiring to be the greatest!

Verse 35: Jesus now spells out in detail a new way of life. In the Kingdom of God the greatest man is not the one who seeks power, leadership and lordship. It is the lowliest servant who is the greatest. We recognize the power struggle on every hand—the desire to be right, to be "one-up" at home, the contest for rating and promotion in business. At school or in church circles or communities, people want to have their way, to set the fashions, to establish trends, to control situations. Jesus cuts right across this pattern of living and models one that is diametrically opposite. We are asked to abandon the play for power and become a servant to our fellows.

Verses 36–37: To love an adult could be to court favor, to gain recognition or distinction. A little child has no favors or privileges to grant. To love a little child is to forego all outward or material returns. One loves for the sheer joy of loving. The return is a joyous heart. To love with no demand for return is to love the person for himself and not for what he can give. This is the way in which God himself loves us.

Verses 38–39: The reason the disciples forbade this man to cast out demons was that he was not "following us"—that is, he did not belong to "our group." Here again is the temptation for power—to control others and make them conform to our patterns of belief and behavior. Jesus drew the inclusive circle of love. Exclusion creates barriers and possible enemies. Inclusion gives hope for friendship. *Verse 40:* Jesus sees in every man the potential for good. He looks at every man with hope and faith.

Verse 41: The water is to be given because "you bear

the name of Jesus," ("belong to Christ," KJV). This may well be an exhortation to us who are within the church graciously to receive favors when offered by those without.

Jesus emphasized rewards. At every turn Jesus points out that his way of life brings great rewards. It was part of his teaching. He that loses his life will find it. If you build your house on the rock, it will stand. You sow seed on good ground and reap thirty, sixty or hundredfold. Yet to follow him for the rewards is to miss the way entirely. The motivation must be that we love God and his children. Any reward comes as a surprise bonus!

QUESTIONS

Verses 30–31: The word *disciple* means "pupil" or "learner." Are you putting the same priority on learning as Jesus did on teaching? Are you satisfied with your understanding of Jesus, with your own life style and the quality of relationship you have with others? What are you doing to learn, to mature, to grow in Christ? Has God any specific direction for you in this?

Verse 31: Do you have any friends or relatives that have a terminal disease? Have you ever been threatened with death? Notice how serenely Jesus went on teaching and loving those bickering disciples even though he was aware his lifetime was limited. Can you carry on like this under stress? Under criticism? Note the faith in God ("after three days will rise") that supported Jesus. How does your faith bear up when outer circumstances look bleak?

Verse 32: Do you shrink back in silent fear, or forth-rightly speak out when confusion and misunderstandings arise? What does this say to you about yourself? *Verse 33:* If there is trouble do you go directly to the heart of it? Is it right sometimes to ignore trouble? Does this say anything to you about yourself?

Verse 34: Do you recognize yourself here? How often I have been silent, not willing to admit I have done something of which I am ashamed. Do you find yourself trapped by little petty quarrels rather than major issues? What are some of the little quarrels or bickerings that beset you? Do you falter before jealousy, gossip, the play for power? In which areas do you need to grow?

Verse 35: Do you see this verse as spelling out the meaning of Jesus' new concept of the Messiah? In the light of this verse, where do we stand? Pulling rank or serving? Demanding rights or pouring out love? Resorting to pressures, overt or subtle, or trusting to caring love?

Verse 36: What a contrast between the *childishness* of the disciples and the *childlike* quality that was in Jesus! Which of these traits do you see in yourself? Do they vary in different situations? At home? In church? On the job? What tends to call forth childish bickering and argument in you? What enables you to move on with childlike teachableness?

Verse 37: Most of us can see God and the Spirit of Jesus in a little child. Can we see God there when the child is irritable and stiffens himself against all efforts to help him? Can we still see God in the child when he grows up to youth, to manhood? Why is it easier to receive a little child than an adult? In what adults are you able or unable to see and love the little child in them? What factors enter in to keep you from welcoming an adult and receiving him as a child of God?

Verse 38: Do you find that you want people to believe and to worship in your way? Do you find yourself wanting to change people who are more conservative or more liberal than you from believing in their way? *Verses 39–40:* Is your conception of church membership such as to include in it people who differ widely in doctrine and practice? Do you really believe in diversity held together by love in an overarching unity? Can you live with people who still have a lot of growing to do, realizing that you, too, need to grow? Talk of this.

Verse 41: Do you find yourself at times being kind or charitable with an unkind or uncharitable spirit? How can you keep the love of Jesus in the Christlike acts? Do you graciously receive love and favors when they come from people with radically different social and ethical standards than yours?

Do you find yourself expecting rewards? To work for a reward is to do it for yourself and not for God. Should hard work in the ranks always be rewarded by presidency or the leadership of the committee or group? Does it hurt when you are not so rewarded? Tell of an experience when you worked for a reward, and of another when you were doing something for sheer joy alone and forgot all about the reward.

20.
EYES, HANDS, AND FEET— WHOSE ARE THEY?

Mark 9:42–50

(42) "Whoever causes one of these little ones who believe in me to sin, it would be better for him if a great millstone were hung round his neck and he were thrown into the sea. (43) And if your hand causes you to sin, cut it off; it is better for you to enter life maimed than with two hands to go to hell, to the unquenchable fire.* (45) And if your foot causes you to sin, cut it off; it is better for you to enter life lame than with two feet to be thrown into hell.* (47) And if your eye causes you to sin, pluck it out; it is better for you to enter the kingdom of God with one eye than with two eyes to be thrown into hell, (48) where their worm does not die, and the fire is not quenched. (49) For every one will be salted with fire. (50) Salt is good; but if the salt has lost its saltness, how will you season it? Have salt in yourselves, and be at peace with one another."

*Verses 44 & 46 (which are identical with verse 48) are omitted by the best authorities.

This section contains a series of independent pithy sayings that stick to the mind as burrs do to cloth. This was a Jewish literary style as we see in the Book of Proverbs. Jesus frequently used this style: e.g., "It is easier for a camel to go through the eye of a needle than for a rich man to enter the kingdom of God" (10:25);

"Whoever loses his life for my sake and the gospel's will save it" (8:35). These sentences (vv. 42–49) are symbolic and to be taken seriously, but not literally. They contain deep truths. Though separate verses use the same word symbols, e.g., salt in both verses 49 and 50, they are not necessarily related to one another.

Verse 42: This is an appeal to help beginning Christians through their awkward, stumbling early steps. It refers to "little ones" in the faith.

Verse 43: There is need for discipline and restraint. If my hand reaches out compulsively for a cigarette or a glass of liquor, it is better to cut cleanly with the habit rather than have my entire life be ruined as I become a chain smoker or an alcoholic. The use of the word *life* here refers to the fullness and joy of living—that life which Jesus offered when he spoke of the life more abundant (John 10:10). *Verse 45:* One is reminded of the Psalmist's words: "The steps of a good man are ordered by the Lord" (Ps. 37:23, KJV).

Verse 47: If my eyes look enviously, greedily, lustfully, and continue to do so, then my whole self will be warped, corrupted, and incapable of appreciating the good and beautiful. The hand, foot and eye represent respectively aggressive, mobile and exploratory parts of our bodies. They reach for power, newness, and intimacy. Life becomes meaningful and effective when these impulses are pursued, but under the discipline of the Master.

Verse 48: "Where decay never stops and the fire never goes out" (Phillips). Sin forever plunders one's personhood and consumes all that is good. It is because of this fact that Jesus came as our Savior. He reveals a God, a

Father, who eternally (in this world and the next) will enfold us with his love making it more and more difficult to refuse him. Nevertheless the decision is always ours, for God will not force his will on us, nor can his forgiveness be effective until we choose to repent.

Verse 49: Moffatt translates this verse, "Everyone has to be consecrated by the fire of the discipline." God's fire is seen in troubles, persecutions, disciplines, reverses. These, without God, can break us; with him, make us. *Verse 50:* We are "the salt of the earth," Jesus said. We are of use to the world only as long as we retain the tang. Good salt becomes worthless if it loses its saltiness, it cannot season anything.

QUESTIONS

It could never be said of Jesus, "He talked too much." Yet how much he said in small compass! Are you too expansive, directive, leaving little to the other fellow's initiative and imagination? How can you so speak as to cultivate creativity and spontaneity in your listener? Note Jesus' use of stories and parables as well as these short sayings.

The Jewish mind constantly thought in symbols that were recognized as such and not taken literally. "The sparrow finds a home . . . where she may lay her young, at thy altars" (Ps. 84:3) suggests a very messy place of worship, if taken literally. The Psalmist however is speaking symbolically of a living God who cares for man even as a mother bird provides for her young.

Do you find that you readily accept the symbolism of the Bible? Can you translate symbolic language like "millstone . . . hung around his neck," "cutting off a hand," "plucking out an eye," "thrown into hell" into Western contemporary thinking *without losing any of the force and urgency* that Jesus intended? Jesus is warning us that sin has dire consequences that defy description. Do these verses convey this to you?

Verse 42: New Christians and beginners in the way of life need tender care and extra patience. Do you tend to be clumsy and thoughtless with them? Or helpful and patient? Do you carelessly expose your own doubts and questions, upsetting them before their faith has taken root?

Verse 43: Is there an incipient habit or weakness in your life that you would be well rid of? What have you done about it? What will you do? The hand takes and touches. Do you find a desire to grasp or touch that which is not yours, either material objects or human?

Verse 45: The foot initiates motion. Is there an inclination on your part to move into destructive habits or behavior—the way you drive, the places you visit, the loitering that delays, the straying and indecision that rob one of purpose?

Verse 47: The eye scans things visible. What do you see? Beauty or so many feet of lumber in a tree? Money that might be yours, or faith, credit and trust in a bank? People as objects to be manipulated, possessed or desired, or persons to be reverenced, enabled, affirmed? What kind of books do you read? When you daydream what kind of things do you experience? Are your "hand,"

114

"foot" and "eye" each under the discipline of God? Speak of these in turn. There is an old English prayer: "God be in my head, and in my understanding. God be in my eyes, and in my looking. God be in my heart, and in my thinking. God be at my end, and in my departing."

Verse 48: A man told me, "I have sinned until I got to the place where I was looking into the jaws of hell. I trembled all over." Is sin repulsive? Does it horrify you? I have to confess that sometimes I eat what I should not, think things I should not, say words that cut and hurt. Sin comes clothed so attractively that I can be enticed and lo! I have slipped before I realize it. Sin needs unmasking! Is this your experience? Share it.

Verse 49: To be a disciple is to accept discipline. They are the same word! The greater the potential in us, the more God tests and tries us—"pruning that we bear more fruit"—in order to bring out the best in us. Isaiah wrote, "Behold, I have refined you . . . I have tried you in the furnace of affliction" (48:10). Tell of some trial you have had. What determined whether it would refine you or embitter you? Were you tempted to blame God, people or yourself? What finally happened?

Verse 50: Once a piece of salt rock has lost its saltiness, it cannot be "resalted." But God's grace is available to us when we fall.

How can a disciple of Jesus regain the "saltiness," the "flavor of Christ"? Do you see this as an occasional periodic process or a continuous procedure?

The final exhortation is to "live at peace with one another" (Weymouth). Do you see peace merely as an absence of discord, a pause between hostilities? Or do you see peace as God's gift in response to our yielding of our own plans and desires to the doing of his will? When was peace just an interlude in your life? When did it become a new spirit given of God enabling you to have an entirely new quality of relationship with other people?

CONCLUSION

The life of Jesus was both unique and universal. This only Son of God has reached the minds and hearts of all of us so that we too may become children of God. We see ourselves mirrored in him, judged, quickened and empowered. We go on our ways renewed and inspired. Life's battle is worthwhile again.

We have felt the spirit of Jesus as he has set his face toward Jerusalem, determined, circumspect, his heart burdened, yet filled with a steadfast, caring love. We have seen how often the disciples disappointed him. We have noted the mounting opposition of the Pharisees. Where will this lead?

Through Suffering to Victory (the next volume in this series) brings the story to its climax: the conflict of minds in questions and debate, the testing of the disciples, the use of stealth and force by Jesus' enemies. The drama of the trial and Calvary is the greatest story ever told, unique and yet universal, as we too are called to share both in his sufferings and his glorious resurrection.